THE JOURNEY

THE CHRONICLES OF A WOMAN APOSTLE

JANICE ARTRY-TURNER

ISBN: 978-1-953048-75-2 (Paperback)

Writers' Branding
1800-608-6550
www.writersbranding.com
orders@writersbranding.com

Contents

Cover Design
by
Terrance Turner II

THIS BOOK IS DEDICATED TO the memory of my dearly loved husband, Ted Willis Turner, Jr., beloved father, Clifford Artry, and my darling mother, Hattie Bell Artry; to my aunts and uncles: Pastor James and Solena Wall (Riverside, California) and Permon and Levada Hankins (Okmulgee, Oklahoma); and to my longest and dearest spiritual mentor, Mother Janie Blake (Riverside, California).

I also dedicate this book to the women around the world who have suffered, are suffering, and will suffer great trials of emotional torture, spiritual persecution, and physical abuse because of their response to the apostolic call of the Lord Jesus Christ.

Under the direction and unction of the Holy Spirit, this book was written to encourage, inspire, and strengthen apostolic women to remind them of the words of our Chief Apostle and Bishop of our souls, Jesus Christ: "Ye have not chosen me, but I have chosen you, and ordained you, that ye should go and bring forth fruit, and that your fruit should remain: that whatsoever ye shall ask of the Father in my name, he may give it you" (John 15:16).

May you forever be faithful and never shrink back from the ministry you have been called into or be ashamed to acknowledge the works, miracles, signs, and wonders God performs through you, which brings honor and glory to Him. Always remember the words of the apostle Paul spoken under the unction of the Holy Ghost: "There is neither Jew nor Greek, there is neither bond nor free, there is neither male nor female: for you are all one in Christ Jesus" (Galatians 3:28).

Mother Janie Blake (Riverside, California), and Dr. Morris Cerullo (Papa) and Mrs. Teresa Cerullo (Mama), (San Diego, CA), who taught Ted and I to be courageous, spiritual warriors in God's army, and released an apostolic anointing for over 35 years, training and inspiring us to step into our ordained spiritual destinies as end-time Apostles for Jesus Christ.

Grace and peace be with you until the coming of our Lord, Jesus Christ.

INTRODUCTION

FOR MORE THAN FIFTY-FIVE YEARS, I have observed the members of the Body of Christ and the interaction between anointed, gifted men and women in denominational and nondenominational churches and faith-based organizations. When I was a young girl, I was occasionally allowed to go to church with relatives and friends. Years later, I was responsible for representing the company I worked for at special celebrations and memorial and funeral services of employees and their family members. God planned my life in such a unique way that I was exposed to and attended services at numerous churches, temples, and synagogues: Pentecostal, Native American Christian, Presbyterian, Baptist, Methodist, Roman Catholic, Nazarene, Full Gospel, Church of God, Church of Christ, Greek Orthodox, Messianic, Orthodox Jewish, Seventh-day Adventist, Reformed Seventh-day Adventist, Sabbath-Keeping Christian, Jehovah's Witness, and Latter-day Saints. The one common denominator I found was that each church, temple, and synagogue claimed to serve God, the Creator of heaven and earth. A few disagreed about the divinity of Jesus Christ and His being the Son of God. Some used other books written by the founders of their church organizations as teachings in addition to the Bible. Others used the Torah, Talmud, or prayer books. However, the most common denominator until recently was the prohibition of women in major decision-making and influential leadership positions in the church or the acknowledgment and acceptance of women with the spiritual gifts of apostles, prophetesses, pastors, evangelists, and teachers within the general assembly. Eddie Hyatt said, "It was only after the church institutionalized and began to think of the apostolic in terms of office and power that women began to be excluded from leadership by men who believed their gender gave them the sole right to lead and rule."[1]

Apostle Paul identified being an apostle as one of the "ministry gifts" given by Jesus for the perfecting of the saints, for the work of the ministry, for the edifying of the body of Christ ..."

In November 2007, I had an encounter with the Holy Spirit in which He revealed that a subtle spirit of confusion and spiritual famine would be in the world. In a night vision, I saw myself holding a Bible. Written on the cover were the words "Holy Bible." I opened the cover of the Holy Bible, and another cover appeared underneath the first cover with the words "New International Bible." I opened that cover, and another book cover appeared with the name of another version, "New Living Translation," and then another translation and another. I never saw the scriptures. I said, "Holy Spirit, what does this mean?"

He said, "In the last days, not many people would be saved from their sins, because man has tampered with the Holy Scriptures and people do not know what to believe."

Shortly after the vision, I noticed more and more English versions of the Bible were showing up in Christian bookstores and online. Frequently, I witnessed the baffled looks on the faces of people whenever a scripture from the King James Version of the Bible was read or quoted because of the lack of knowledge of this authorized version of the Bible. In today's churches, is it exceptional when congregations read scriptures in unison during a worship service from their Bibles. Bible passages are projected on a screen in many churches today because of the many English versions of the Bible circulating in the world.

The Holy Spirit led me to write on this particular topic because I am a female disciple and minister of Jesus Christ. I am a woman with more than fifty years of exciting experience in ministry. God called, chose, and ordained me as an end-time apostle (sent one). I am simply dust that God breathed on and gave life to proclaim the "good news" to spiritually dead people. I am thankful for the Lord putting spiritual generals in my life, men and women who discerned God's call on my life, spoke into my life, laid hands on me, and encouraged me to seek the counsel of God through consecration, fasting, praying, and studying scriptures.

Realizing the valuable resources available from academic preparation for effective evangelism in the end times, I am a lifetime student of the Bible and study other disciplines that influence the beliefs, values, and morals of present and future generations. I was blessed to earn education degrees from Southern Illinois University at Carbondale and California Baptist University in education, BS and a MS. I also attended Arkansas Baptist College, Bethel Christian College, and Victory Bible Institute.

In 1993, I was called by God into full-time ministry as a pastor and church planter. I cofounded Truth Ministries Church in Beaumont, California, a nondenominational, Spirit-filled, Bible-based Christian ministry. In 1993, I was ordained as an administrator by the Church of God in Christ in Jurisdiction #2. In 1994, I was ordained and consecrated as a reverend and pastor by the Mount Zion Lighthouse Full-Gospel Church. In 1989, I was introduced to Morris Cerullo World Evangelism and became a partner, student, and supportive member of the board of elders.

The Holy Spirit inspired the writing of this book for the exposing of an ancient demonic spirit that is hindering the propagation of disciples of Jesus Christ, the proclamation of the kingdom of God, and the finished redemptive work of Jesus Christ on the cross. God's will has always been to have fellowship with His choicest creation, humankind. However, Satanic influences in the form of worldly-wise intellectual deception infiltrated the hearts and minds of men and women in the churches around the world. Consequently, shame and reproach have been brought upon the name of Jesus Christ by those who claim to represent God and Jesus Christ of the Holy Scriptures. It has fueled the pernicious spirit of unbelief and lack of confidence in the message of forgiveness of sin and salvation through the death and resurrection of Jesus Christ. There is only one solution: acknowledgment of sin against the will of God that none perish, repentance for hindering called-to-leadership positions in the church and other ministries, and, last but not least, the humble submission of hearts and wills to God, thereby bringing reconciliation between the conspirators and God and those impacted by their destructive behavior.

Once the spirit of "female exclusiveness" in ministry is bound and cast out of the churches all over the world, the flames of evangelism will ignite the hearts of God's people in such an unimaginable way the chaff of antagonism, segregation, racism, discrimination, spiritual humiliation, harassment, and spiritual abuse will be consumed, liberating the wheat that it might grow unhindered. Then once again, the glorious, powerful church Jesus Christ built will witness the dynamic presence of the Holy Ghost falling from heaven like a rushing mighty wind, ushering sinners to the altars. Unbelievers will fall on their knees, crying out, "What must I do to be saved?" The Body of Christ is in the earth to fulfill God's will, leading people to Jesus Christ, that they might escape the wrath and judgment that is coming upon the earth, that they would live a life of faith, experience inner peace, and spend eternity with God in the New Jerusalem. The central theme of this book is oneness in the Body of Christ. I am an apostle of Jesus Christ sent with this message to the whole Body of Christ. Jesus said, "That they all may be one; as thou, Father, art in me, and I in thee, that they also may be one in us; *that the world may believe that thou hast sent me*" (John 17:21, emphasis added).

DIVINE PROTECTION

WHEN I WAS A SMALL child, I sensed what I later learned were angels visiting me. I was terrified when they revealed themselves to me. I'd run out of the room screaming, "Someone's in my room!" My sisters looked under the bed and in the closet assuring me there was no one in the room. I was not consoled at all. I knew what I saw, and I was afraid to be alone. I stayed close to my parents or sisters.

Eventually, my mama realized angels were visiting me. She tried to comfort me by saying, "Jan, don't be afraid. God sent the angels to protect and watch over you, not to hurt you."

Quite naturally, my sisters thought I was making it up for attention. They gazed at me with incredulous looks each time I told them I saw angels. I thought to myself, *I sure wish my sisters could see them. They think I'm just acting out*—which I did a lot. After all, I was the baby. But I was the only one the angels would reveal themselves to. Of course, nothing anyone could say would console me. I was happy I didn't have my own bed. My sisters grudgingly allowed me into theirs. However, they could only put up with me for a couple of nights because I was a wiggler.

Years later, I had my own room and my own bed. The angels sang to me, and I in turn would sing the songs the next morning at the breakfast table. My mother was right; they gently watched over me. I soon became aware they were sent not to harm me but to comfort and protect me. I know this may sound strange to some of you, but the Bible confirms God assigns angels to every child born.

Jesus said, "Take heed that ye despise not one of these little ones; for I say unto you, That in heaven their angels do always behold the face of my Father which is in heaven" (Matthew 18:10). Did you realize every one of you reading this book also has guardian angels watching over you? You may not be able to see them, but they are there. I often thought about why I was allowed to see the angels, but after I became more spiritually mature, I realized God wanted me to know I would never be alone and would always be protected.

From the beginning of my earliest memories, I was familiar with the name of Jesus Christ. He was a member of our household. Placards with scriptures hung on the wall; a cross and pictures of the Last Supper and Jesus knocking at a door were imprinted in my mind. I recall kneeling and praying with my mom, dad, and sister in the morning and at night. I really looked forward to nighttime prayers because I was a real scaredy-cat. As a family, we ate our meals together, saying grace before, and attended church two to three times a week. I was born into a Christian home that provided a sense of security, love, and well-being.

My mom was a singer-songwriter and worked at a glove factory. We all enjoyed singing. We all had lovely voices. Hymns and gospel music regularly filled our home. Mom would read Bible stories to me, and I always enjoyed sharing what I had learned with others. I would eagerly repeat the stories to anyone who would listen.

I was the seventh child of six girls and one boy: Rozina (Rose), Katherine (Kat), Luther (Sonny), Ernestine (Stein), Cliford Jean (Jean), Elaine (Laine), and me, Janice (Jan). Perhaps God was leading my mother to instill the message of Jesus's love and protection in my heart because she would pass away from cancer a month after my seventh birthday at the age of thirty-nine. It was over sixty years before I realized how much my parents really loved me and what a difficult decision they faced when Mom was no longer able to care for me. I can only imagine, after much prayer and discussion with the extended family members, how difficult it was for my parents to separate me from the rest of the family. But they finally decided the best place was with my father's sister and her family in Oklahoma. But unlike today, when parents ask children's opinion about where they want to stay, what they want to eat, or what they want to wear, in the early fifties, parents were the decision makers. I was only five years old. I had no idea of where I was going or why. I only knew I was going on a trip with my dad and sisters.

After traveling what seemed like forever, we finally reached our destination. I was quite stunned by all the green trees surrounding the house and the strange smells and sounds. I had never seen such a place. The weather was hot and muggy, and dust was flying as we headed to our destination on the dirt road. When we arrived, a short, pleasant-looking woman saw us driving toward the house, promptly stopped what she was doing, and briskly walked toward us with a broad smile on her face as she approached the car. My dad warmly embraced her. She was introduced to me as Aunt Levada, Dad's sister. She seemed so happy to see us. She hugged and kissed each of us, and I liked her from the moment I saw her. A tall, slender man was behind her, and he also warmly greeted us. He greeted my dad, and I heard him call him "brother," which meant he was my dad's brother-in-law. Then I saw a boy and a girl running toward the car. They introduced themselves as our cousins, Ruby and Charles (Plucky). Ruby was six, and Plucky was four. They seemed friendly, and I was happy to have someone close to my age to play with.

Everything was drastically different from what I was familiar with. I had never been on a real farm with horses, cows, chickens, ducks, and a country watchdog. It was quite a culture shock. Dad had occasionally taken me to Knott's Berry Farm to ride the ponies, but it was nothing compared to this place. The house was close to a river, and mosquitoes buzzed around us, seeking fresh California blood. The kids warned us not to walk in tall grass because of ticks. Of course, I had no idea of what they were talking about. I had never heard of any bloodsucking insects. I saw snakes crawling across the dusty road and slithering through the grass. At nightfall, everything was pitch-black. My aunt cooked a delicious meal on an old cast-iron wood burning stove. We spent the evening talking as the oil lamp cast shadows on the walls of the house. It was a small white house with a wooden front porch and one concrete step. To our—except for Dad's—surprise, there was no inside plumbing, so during the day, we went to a small wooden building called an outhouse to use the bathroom. During the night, we used a white enamel container with a red ring and a white top on it, called a slop jar. My sisters thought everything was disgusting, but I was fascinated by how unique things were. I especially enjoyed priming the pump and watching the water come out during the day and at night staring at the dazzling stars in the pitch black sky. Because of the profound darkness, the brilliant light of the moon and stars was magnificent, and it was so serene.

The sad day came when my excitement turned to befuddlement and somberness. My dad and sisters returned to California and left me behind. They left while I was sleeping. I am sure my dad knew I would pitch a fit if they had tried to leave without me. When I asked my aunt where my dad and sisters were, she told me they had returned to California. My heart began to pound, and I was afraid. I began to cry uncontrollably, looking down the road, hoping to catch a glimpse of them coming back to get me. I did not understand what was happening. I was in a strange place with unfamiliar people.

I cried and prayed, "God, please send my dad back to take me home. I want my mama and daddy."

For days, I did not eat and cried myself to sleep. I missed my sisters, brother, and other relatives. Everyone tried to comfort me, but I just wanted to go home. I never expressed what I was thinking; neither did I talk. I saw the concerned looks on the faces of my aunt and uncle, and I was remorseful for the distress I caused. I soon discovered I was not the only child with a broken heart. My cousins told me they too felt sad. Their mothers had moved to California and left them with their grandparents. That told me they understood how lonely I felt without my family. Hearing that made me feel a little better, knowing they missed their mothers also, although I believed my situation was quite different from theirs. As time went on, I began to adjust to the fact this would be my home for a while. I was with family, and they would take good care of me. They were soft-spoken and patient. There was no doubt in my mind they loved me.

I quickly adjusted to living on a farm. We went to bed early and woke up early. I learned to chop wood, feed (slop) hogs, pump water, gather eggs, feed chickens, ride horses, and help make tea cakes. Despite knowing I was loved, safe, and taken care of, I missed my family. I was terribly homesick. As long as I was busy working, I didn't think much about going home, but at night, I still cried myself to sleep. My nerves were bad, and my hair started falling out. Large patches of hair would come out from the scalp each time my aunt ran the comb through my hair. Eventually, there were only a few long strands left on the top of my head. I was despondent, and Ruby would comment about the doleful look on my face. What sustained me was remembering what my mom had said about Jesus loving me and never leaving me.

I could see the worry on my aunt's face as she watched my hair fall out and saw my sad countenance. Early one morning, I heard a car drive up to the house. To my surprise, it was my daddy. I ran to the car as fast as I could and jumped into his arms. It was such a jubilant day. I thought to myself, *At last, I am going home!* The next morning before daybreak, we were on our way to California. The closer we got, the more excited I became. I thought about how it would feel to have my mother's arms around me again.

Once we arrived, I jumped out of the car and ran into her outstretched arms. I sat on her lap and felt her warm embrace and gentle kisses on my cheeks. I was elated to once again touch, kiss, and hug my mama. I had missed seeing her beautiful face and lovely smile. I never wanted to ever leave her again. Then I looked into her eyes, and she didn't look the same. She was sick, frail, pale, and sitting in a wheelchair, unable to stand or walk. It never entered my mind that she would be the one who would leave next, never to return to our earthly home. She was going to be in the presence of the Lord.

My mom was a praying woman and full of faith. Every day, she prayed over my head and massaged ointment into my scalp. While she was massaging, she would say, "Jan, God is going to grow your hair back." Just as she said, in a couple of months, I had a full head of hair.

The women of the church were a blessing to our family. Daily, they came to our house to take care of me and my mother. On one particular day, one of the women took my sisters and me to her house. I didn't know Mom's condition had turned grave. I heard my sisters crying. I asked them what was wrong, and they said, "Mama's gone." I really did not know what they meant, and when we returned home, Mom wasn't there. Frequently, she would go to the hospital and stay for a while and then would return home. I thought that was where she was. However, she never came home. The next time I saw her was at the funeral. Once again, I had been separated from my mother, and I felt so all alone. Shortly after Mom went to be with Jesus, I returned to Oklahoma to my aunt and uncle's, where I stayed for the next five years.

While I was in California, natural gas was discovered on my uncle's property, and they built a little larger home closer to town but still in the country. I was glad when I returned and we had gas and electricity. But there seemed to be more work than before. My uncle planted acres of corn and cotton and owned over a hundred head of cattle. I worked in the fields and chopped and picked cotton and corn, in addition to other farm chores. We grew all our food and raised all our livestock. After dinner and all the chores were done, I found solace in the scriptures and prayed earnestly to someday return home. Although I spent time reading the Bible, singing songs from the hymnal, and knew about Jesus, I had never had a personal experience with him. Mama taught me to reverently kneel when I prayed. I recalled the day Mama said, "Jan, ask Jesus to come into your heart." I obeyed, but I didn't really understand what salvation meant. I knew He heard me though because I believed everything she told me about Jesus.

I was blessed to see my family yearly. Every summer, Dad hired a young lady named Doll to escort me on the train from Oklahoma to California, where I would spend two months with my family and other relatives. I looked forward to spending time with them. Los Angeles was a whole new world compared to where I was living. I felt strange and disconnected from my sisters because I could not relate to their free lifestyles and the way they talked. I had acquired an "Okie" accent, and my vocabulary was unlike theirs. I would say "draw the water" when referring to running water into the bathtub. I was accustomed to letting a bucket down into a well to draw water. Therefore, my language was more descriptive. I was petite and rather skinny. I wanted my sisters to like me, so I would act like a clown by dancing around and being silly, and they would laugh at me. When Mom was alive, she never allowed worldly music or dancing in our home, but all that changed when she was no longer there to monitor the activities in the home. I'd watch my sisters dancing along with the dancers on the Dick Clark show on television and try to imitate them, but I wasn't very good at it, and they would crack up.

It was during one of those summer visits to California when my life was dramatically transformed. On a Sunday morning, Daddy and I went to Sunday school. After Sunday school, someone always gave an overview of the lesson. While I listened to the Sunday school review, the Spirit of the Lord came upon me, and tears began to roll down my cheeks. For the first time, I felt a wonderful presence overshadow me. I felt at peace and loved. I was experiencing the love of Jesus Mama had told me about.

The man said, "Jesus loved you so much He was willing to voluntarily suffer and die to take away all your sin forever."

All my life, I'd attended church but had never experienced anything so glorious. My eyes were closed, and I heard voices telling me, "Ask Jesus to forgive your sins and to come into your life." I was aware members of the church were standing around me, but it was as though I was in another place because of the overwhelming peace and love I was experiencing. I heard a voice say, "Ask Jesus to forgive your sins and to come into your life as your Savior."

That day, I asked Jesus to be my Savior, and oh, how indescribable was the joy that filled my soul. Suddenly, my crying turned into shouts of praise. I shouted, "Thank You, Jesus! Thank You for loving me, forgiving me, and saving me!"

Afterward, the minister asked me to tell the congregation about what had happened to me. I rose from where I was sitting and walked to the front of the church. There was a deafening silence in the building. I looked at all the smiling faces with their eyes staring at me, and I shouted, "I am saved! Jesus saved me!"

They all stood to their feet, clapped their hands, and shouted, "Hallelujah! Glory to *God*!"

I was born into a tight-knit extended family. We did everything together and took care of each other's needs. This closeness even included sharing children with couples who did not have them. Mom was the youngest of five siblings. She had three children from a previous marriage and four girls with Dad. She was blessed with six girls and one boy. Mom's sister, Aunt Willie Francis, and Uncle Henry had no children. Mom and Dad agreed to allow them to raise my brother. Aunt Solena and Uncle James had two sons and were unable to have any more children. According to the story I was told, before I was born, my mom and dad agreed to let Aunt Solena and Uncle James raise me. When I was a couple of months old, Mom and Dad presented me to my aunt and uncle by placing me in Aunt Solena's arms and saying, "Here is your daughter, Sol."

However, just as they were about to walk out the door, Dad turned around and said, "I can't leave my baby down here."

They took me back to Los Angeles with the understanding Aunt Solena and Uncle James would see me every week, which they did until Mom became ill with cancer and I was taken to Oklahoma.

My uncle pastored a small church, and when I told him and Aunt Solena about the wonderful experience I'd had, they were overjoyed to hear I was saved. When I was with them, I felt loved and secure. I knew they loved me very much, and I loved them too.

The summer of 1956, when I was ten years old, Uncle James, who called me "Champion," asked me to teach the younger kids' Sunday school class at the Eleventh Street Church of God in Christ, later named St. James. He knew my love for the Bible and how I enjoyed sharing stories from it. This indeed was a dream come true for me. I loved the thought of reading Bible stories to the younger kids and teaching them to pray and to sing songs about Jesus. That was the beginning of my ministry as a teacher of the Word of God. As far back as I can recall, my mother read the Bible to me every day, and she taught me to read from the Bible before I was five years old.

My heavenly Father had preordained me as a teacher of His Word before I was in my mother's womb. The Bible says, "Lo, Children are a heritage of the Lord: and the fruit of the womb is his reward" (Psalm 127:3). God said of Jeremiah, "Before I formed thee in the belly I knew thee ..." (Jeremiah 1:5).

Regardless of the circumstances surrounding a child's conception and birth, God created the child and has a purpose for bringing forth that life. No conception or birth is ever an accident.

> Pilate questioned Jesus about his identity. He said, "Art thou a king then?" Jesus answered, "Thou says that I am a king. To this end was I born, and for this cause came I into the world, that I should bear witness unto the truth. Every one that is of the truth heareth my voice." (John 18:37)

It is a frightening thought that Judas Iscariot was born to betray the Messiah. When Jesus prayed in John 17, he referred to Judas as "the son of perdition." *Thayer's Greek Lexicon*, Strong NT 684, defines *perdition* in reference to John 17:12 as (apo'leia) "destruction, loss, ruin, perishing, eternal ruin; the destruction which consists in the loss of eternal life, eternal misery, perdition, the lot of those excluded from the kingdom of God."

Jesus prayed, "While I was with them in the world, I kept them in thy name: those that thou gavest me I have kept, and none of them is lost, but the son of perdition; that the scripture might be fulfilled" (John 17:12).

The scripture Jesus referred to is in the book of Zechariah. Zechariah was an Old Testament prophet who lived in the sixth century. God revealed to Zechariah the specific details of the betrayal of the Messiah. "And I said unto them, good, give me my price; and if not, forbear. So, they weighed for my price thirty pieces of silver. And I took the thirty pieces of silver, and cast them to the potter in the house of the Lord" (Zechariah 11:12–13).

The prophecy in Zechariah was fulfilled in the book of Matthew.

> Then one of the twelve, called Judas Iscariot, went unto the chief priests, and said unto them, "What will ye give me, and I will deliver him unto you?" And they covenanted with him for thirty pieces of silver. And from that time, he sought opportunity to betray him [Jesus, the Messiah]. (Matthew 26:14–16)

Sorrowful, Judas returned the money.

> Then Judas, which had betrayed him, when he saw that he was condemned, repented himself, and brought again the thirty pieces of silver to the chief priest and elders, saying, I have sinned in that I betrayed the innocent blood. And they said, What is that to us? see thou to that. And he cast down the pieces of silver in the temple, and departed, and went and hanged himself. (Matthew 27:3–5)

What a sad event. It was not just a coincidence Judas betrayed Jesus; that was his ordained destiny, just as Jeremiah was ordained to be a prophet of God. God said, "Before I formed thee in the belly I knew thee, and before thou camest forth out of the womb I sanctified thee, and I ordained thee a prophet unto the nations" (Jeremiah 1:5).

Isaiah was born to be a prophet of God. Isaiah described his call to the service of the Lord: "Then I heard the voice of the Lord saying, 'Whom shall I send? And who will go for us?' And I said, 'Here am I, Send me'" (Isaiah 6:9).

Like the prophets and patriarchs of the Bible, God called me, and I said, "Here am I; send me." I've always sensed the presence of God in my life even before I totally surrendered my life to the Lord. I've always wanted to work for the Lord but was hearing conflicting voices, which delayed my stepping into my ordained purpose. For years, I wandered around doing a lot of "good things," thinking I was in the will of God. Once I discovered God's purpose for my life, a peace and rest came over my soul that transcends all human understanding.

Ruby, Plucky, and I were responsible for supplying the household water. Daily, we walked an eighth of a mile to the Creek Nation Christian Church, filled our buckets with well water, and carried it back to our house. Once a month, my aunt cooked for the church, and we spent time playing with the kids while she prepared the meals. Weekly, we participated in their youth activities, and one Saturday, we attended a youth service at the campgrounds. I saw a movie about how God used the prophet Elisha to restore life to a boy who had died.

The miracle portrayed on the screen introduced me to a supernatural God who uses people to accomplish His purposes upon the earth. After the movie, I rushed home, found the scriptures about the miraculous event, and read them over and over.

> And when Elisha was come into the house, behold, the child was dead and laid upon his bed. He went in therefore, and shut the door upon them, and prayed unto the Lord. And he went up, and lay upon the child, and put his mouth upon his mouth, and his eyes upon his eyes, and

> his hands upon his hands: and he stretched himself upon the child; and the flesh of the child waxed warm. Then he returned, and walked in the house to and fro; and went up, and stretched himself upon him: and the child sneezed seven times, and the child opened his eyes. And he called Gehazi and said, Call this Shunammite. So, he called her. And when she was come in unto him, he said, Take up thy son. Then she went in, and fell at his feet, and bowed herself to the ground and took up her son, and went out. (2 Kings 4:32–37)

God used that movie to introduce me to the one and only supernatural God, who performs extraordinary miracles through human beings. That night, I knelt beside my bed and asked God to use me like He used Elisha. Of course, I did not know the suffering that accompanies such a powerful anointing. I witnessed a compassionate, loving God, who is concerned about a broken heart. I saw how brokenhearted the mother was at the death of her child and the joy she expressed when she saw that her son was alive. I later learned the ministering gifts of the Holy Spirit will only work by the counsel of God and as He wills. Elisha was not acting on his own accord but was a vessel used by God to accomplish God's purpose. Elisha prayed, listened, and followed God's instructions. Death was denied the life of the child. Breath entered his lungs, and he was restored back to his beloved mother.

FRIENDLY FIRE

GROWING UP, I OFTEN WONDERED why I never saw women standing on the raised platform behind the pulpit when teaching scriptures or praying. They were permitted to stand on the floor behind a table in front of the platform. I observed many anointed women who fervently prayed and proclaimed the gospel of Jesus Christ. I heard their passionate prayers, beheld their pleasant conduct, and witnessed their love for God and their brothers and sisters in Christ and their obedience to leadership. I realized much later it was an unspoken law that women could not be appointed as elders, ministers, pastors, or key leaders over the general assembly in the church. They were permitted to serve in other capacities, but the clergy was a "male" position only.

The more I studied scriptures, the more I desired to have a more intimate relationship with God and to know and follow the teachings of Jesus. I was saved at ten years old and baptized in water but was not baptized with the Holy Ghost and fire until I was twenty-two. God's anointing was upon me, and He had given me such compassion and love for those who were sick and those bound and oppressed by the devil. I had a burning desire to win souls, to lead them to Jesus, knowing once they experienced His healing touch, their lives would never be the same. I wanted to use my body to accomplish His will to save, heal, and set captives free, so in faith, I laid hands on the sick, and they were healed by Jesus. I had little interest in other things. I completely surrendered my life to Jesus. When I prayed for people, the Holy Spirit would reveal to me the exact place where they had pain. Then the women in the church began to tell me that I was trying to be "a wonder." That was a term used for a person who by faith really believed he or she could do what the Bible said people could do in the name of Jesus. Well, I believed the Bible and surrendered my body to the Holy Spirit to work through me, and He did the work. I heard this negative, faith-busting, binding message each time someone testified about how God had healed him or her in response to faith-filled prayer or delivered when I exercised the authority of Jesus's name to bind up and cast out the wicked demonic spirits. Satan wanted people to be sick and bound by demonic activities, so he used my brothers and sisters in Christ to try to discourage me with their sarcastic words. Yes, I was very young, but I could not just see people suffering when I knew Jesus died to set them free and He wanted to use my body, my voice, and my hands to accomplish His will concerning them. It did not stop me, but I stopped ministering publicly and ministered privately to avoid the persecution. After praying for people, I would tell them, "I believe God heard our prayers, but please don't tell anyone I prayed for you." I didn't want to quench the Holy Spirit, but I found it challenging to exercise the ministry gifts in an environment of skepticism and unbelief. I was taught to reverently fear God and to obey the leading of the Holy Spirit. The apostle Paul addressed this same matter of faithfulness in the service of the Lord when he said, "Quench not the Spirit" (1 Thessalonians 5:19).

My spirit was grieved and bound by the traditions and doctrines of men. This hindering spirit brought a spirit of confusion upon me because the Bible was saying one thing and the women and men in the church were saying something contrary to what I was reading. Not only did I feel confused, but a spirit of discouragement was trying to overtake me. I was young and lacked knowledge of how to take an offensive position against the devil. I did not know anything about spiritual warfare. The comments of the older women in the church wounded me. The sermons I heard encouraged me to say yes to the Lord. But the voices from those around me were telling me, "You need to wait on your calling, as a helpmate. God does not call women to preach, but they can speak. Women are not to lay hands on people. That's a man's job."

Despite what they said to me, I knew what Jesus had said. He said, "Behold, I give unto you power to tread on serpents and scorpions, and over all the power of the enemy: and nothing shall by any means hurt you" (Luke 10:19).

> Go into all the world, and preach the gospel to every creature ... And these signs shall follow them that believe; In my name shall they cast out devils; they shall speak with new tongues ... They shall take up serpents; and if they drink any deadly thing, it shall not hurt them; they shall lay hands on the sick and they shall recover. (Mark 16:15, 17–18)

God expects every believer, not just leaders, to allow the Holy Spirit to flow through them in the churches and in their communities, to bind and cast out devils, and to set people free in Jesus's name. I stirred the gifts up by consecrating (setting myself apart from worldly activities), praying, and fasting. I studied faith-building scriptures and read biographies of spirit filled, wholly dedicated Christians. I became encouraged, and my faith in God and His Word grew stronger. God was grooming me for the ministry gift He would one day bestow upon me. I learned in my frail humanity I was no match for the devil, but the Spirit of the Holy Ghost and the resurrected power of Jesus Christ would work through me to accomplish God's purpose. The Holy Spirit revealed to me that the battle was not my battle but the Lord's. The battle is not yours either; it's the Lord's. When it seemed overwhelming because of the many spiritual attacks against me, I found great consolation in the writings of Apostle Paul.

> What shall we then say to these things? If God be for us, who can be against us? He that spared not his own Son, but delivered him up for us all, how shall he not with him also freely give us all things? Who shall lay anything to the charge of God's elect? It is God that justified. Who is he that condemneth? It is Christ that died, yea rather, that is risen again, who is even at the right hand of God, who also maketh intercession for us. Who shall separate us from the love of Christ? Shall tribulation, or distress, or persecution, or famine, or nakedness, or peril, or sword? As it is written, For thy sake we are killed all the day long; we are accounted as sheep for the slaughter. Nay, in all these things we are more than conquerors through him that loved us. For I am persuaded, that neither death, nor

> life, nor angels, nor principalities, nor powers, nor things present, nor things to come, nor height, nor depth, nor any other creature shall be able to separate us from the love of God, which is in Christ Jesus our Lord. (Romans 8:31–39)

The Holy Spirit revealed to me the devil is literally using other believers in the churches to practice "spiritual abortion." There are many female apostles, prophets, pastors, evangelists, and teachers sitting in church pews out of the will of God. Some have gone back into the world because someone was influenced by a demonic spirit to hinder or kill the gift. The apostle Paul admonished young Timothy, in 2 Timothy 1:6, 7, to stir up his spiritual gift: "Wherefore I put thee in remembrance that thou stir up the gift of God, which is in thee by the putting on of my hands. For God hath not given us the spirit of fear; but of power and of love, and of a sound mind."

Oh, how I wished I had that type of encouragement when God began using me as a young woman. Despite the discouraging comments, the Holy Spirit gave me a gift that I am keenly aware belongs to God. He expected me to be a good steward over the gift. God gave me the gift of the Holy Ghost to bless humanity and to bring glory to His Name. I truly love the Lord, and I am thankful for Him choosing me to be one of millions who are continuing Jesus's work upon the earth. I fear being an unprofitable, lazy servant. Because I reverently fear the Lord, I dare not settle for a life of ease or leisure. There are too many souls to reach, too many people waiting for someone to introduce them to their Savior, too many infirm, sick, and feeling hopeless. God gives gifts to Christians to profit all people, not just other Christians. This too is a misconception among believers. They only minister to members of their own church or other Christians. Jesus addressed this mind-set in Matthew 9 and 1 Corinthians 12:7.

> And as Jesus passed forth from thence, he saw a man named Matthew, sitting at the receipt of custom: and he saith unto him, Follow me. And it came to pass, as Jesus sat at meat in the house, behold, many publicans and sinners came and sat down with him and his disciples. And when the Pharisees saw it, they said unto his disciples,

> Why eateth your Master with publicans and sinner? But when Jesus heard that, he said unto them, They that be whole need not a physician, but they that are sick. But go ye and learn what that meaneth, I will have mercy, and not sacrifice: for I am not come to call the righteous, but sinners to repentance. (Matthew 9:9–13)

"But the manifestation of the Spirit is given to every man to profit withal" (1 Corinthians 12:7).

Not only does the Body of Christ profit, but the people in the world do as well. "For God so loved the world, that he gave his only begotten Son that whosoever believeth in him should not perish but have everlasting life" (John 3:16).

God has not changed his mind about the love he has for the people in the world. Jesus saves us for the purpose of telling everyone we come in contact with about what He accomplished at Calvary; as the Lamb of God, Jesus bore the sins of every human being who would ever live, cleansing us from sin forever when He hung on the cross. Jesus's death satisfied the wrath of God that was against mankind because of our disobedience, restoring our relationship with our Creator and heavenly Father. Jesus's death gave us all access to our Creator God. Jesus's bruises, stripes, and shed blood healed our sick souls and bodies. Jesus rising from the dead gave us everlasting life, and an immortal body awaits us.

The devil does not want the people in the world to hear this message. The devil's purpose is to convince people he does not exist, God does not exist, there is no such thing as sin or judgment and no heaven or hell, and Jesus is not the Son of God, born of a virgin, or that He lived a sinless life and is alive, sitting on the right hand of His father in heaven but coming again to earth. Satan and his demons influence people to stay in their sin and continue a destructive lifestyle leading to an early death from drunkenness, suicide, murder, lewdness, addiction, sexual immorality, perversion, ungodliness, and wickedness in order to possess their souls, securing them with deception and lies that they may spend eternity fully conscious of no return from a fiery, tormenting abyss called hell or Hades.

A well-known, respected end-time prophet and apostle Morris Cerullo shared at one of his conferences about the closing of a school for the deaf because God's people believed they served a supernatural, creative God who could cause the deaf to hear. Think of all the hospitals, jails, nursing homes, and mental institutions that would shut down if every disciple of Christ would believe and act on the Word of God. If they would rid themselves of secret sin and iniquity, totally surrendering their lives and wills to the Father, then the manifested power of God would flow through them and He would use them to work the works of God. Multitudes would come into the kingdom of God, and sick bodies and souls would be healed. The Body of Christ has the answer to the major problems facing our world. The Body of Christ is well equipped to finish the work we have begun, but we must not forget the answer Jesus gave to His disciples when they asked Him a very important question in John 6: "What shall we do, that we might work the works of God?" (John 6:28).

"And Jesus answered and said unto them. This is the work of God, that ye believe on him whom he hath sent. All that the Father giveth me shall come to me; and him that cometh to me I will in no wise cast out" (John 6: 29, 37).

Jesus sent the Holy Ghost to abide inside of believers for the purpose of manifesting the same power, the same authority, and the same anointing that came down from heaven to heal a sick world over two thousand years ago. When I confess that I am a member of the Body of Christ, I am to be identified as a "miracle worker," just like Jesus, and even greater works are to be manifested through my life as promised by Jesus before He left the earth.

Jesus said, "Verily, verily, I say unto you, He that believeth on me, the works that I do shall he do also; greater works than these shall he do; because I go unto my Father" (John 14:12).

Because of persecution and rejection by families, friends, and the church, the majority of people going to church and hearing messages about miracles, signs, and wonders think to themselves, *How wonderful it was for God to use the disciples, apostles, prophets, and members of the early church, but He is not doing that now.* Nothing is further from the truth. Later in the book, I will share about incredible, supernatural, miraculous healings, divine interventions, and deliverances I have personally witnessed God perform. I am grateful to the Lord for entrusting me with such a precious gift as an apostle of Jesus Christ. I dare not take the gift for granted or consider it my own.

In 1995, I came across an article in a local newspaper about a mother whose son was involved in an accident and had been in a coma for over eight years. The Holy Spirit instructed me to arrange for the ministers in our church to go to the hospital for the purpose of ministering to comatose patients. By faith, we went to the hospital and followed the specific instructions of the Holy Spirit. We witnessed the most incredible, unexplainable supernatural, miraculous healings of patients with brain abnormalities. Women and men were suddenly waking up after being in comas for years. Tracheotomy tubes were being removed, and patients were discharged from the hospitals. It was an amazing thing to witness. Each month, we visited the hospital, and we inquired about a patient we had ministered to the previous month and were told the patient had returned home.

Solomon said in Proverbs 17:8, "A gift is as a precious stone in the eyes of him that hath it: whithersoever it turneth, it prospereth."

Jesus is that precious gift. When He is present, everything changes for good. He is waiting for His people to ask for the healing anointing. I know what it is like to suffer with pain in your body, to experience depression and grief, and to be dependent on others. When you are a believer in Christ, suffering produces compassion and empathy. When you are suffering, you need someone who can believe with you for your deliverance, healing, or breakthrough. I've been challenged with health issues, and my brothers and sisters in Christ were aware of them but failed to pray for me to receive my healing.

I said to the Lord, "Where are Your people who are hearing and believing Your Word?"

The next day, I received a call from a Christian woman from Chicago and another call from my spiritual son from Texas. Both of these followers of Christ said, "The Lord put you on my heart, and I had to stop and call you and to pray for you." If there was ever any doubt that there are true believers on the earth who are communing with God, this experience proved to me there are men and women who are in an intimate relationship with God, who not only hear the voice of God but are obedient. After I received the calls and they agreed with me for my healing according to Matthew 18:19, the infirmity left my body. Jesus said, "Again, I say unto you, That if two of you shall agree on earth as touching anything that they shall ask, it shall be done for them of my Father which is in heaven."

We don't have to look any further than Jesus Christ to know how to effectively use the gifts God bestowed upon us. Jesus had compassion for people. He loved them, and He knew why He was born. He declared it openly: "I was sent to preach the gospel to the poor; heal the brokenhearted, preach deliverance to the captives, recovering of sight to the blind and to set at liberty them that are bruised" (Luke 4:18).

The church, the Body of Christ, is in the earth to duplicate the works of Jesus.

GLIMPSE OF HEAVEN

IN 1988, GOD CHANGED THE course of my life when a coworker said, "Ms. Turner, have you ever heard of Morris Cerullo World Evangelism?"

I said, "No, who and what is that?"

He said, "He is a prophet and evangelist, and his ministry is in other countries. He will be conducting a world conference at the Anaheim Hilton Hotel this weekend. You may want to go."

I kept thinking about our conversation, and the Holy Spirit led me to go on a Saturday morning. I had no idea of what to expect. I just felt the Holy Spirit luring me to go and see. When I opened the door of the ballroom, it was as if I had been transported to the kingdom of God. I saw and heard the most heavenly sights and sounds I had ever seen or heard. I saw thousands of people from different nations with their hands lifted upward toward heaven. I heard them praising God in their heavenly language. From that moment on, my perspective about the church of the Lord Jesus Christ dramatically changed. I witnessed people of various skin tones, from different nations, kindreds, and tongues crying out corporately to the God of all creation. They were dressed in their international clothing, worshipping, blessing, and honoring Jesus.

> And they sung a new song, saying, Thou art worthy to take the book, and to open the seals thereof: for thou was slain, and hast redeemed us to God by the blood out of every kindred, and tongue, and people, and nation; And hast made us unto our God kings and priest: and we shall reign on the earth. (Revelation 5:9–10)

Then the Holy Spirit said, "This is what Heaven will be like." After that glorious experience, my perspective on the Lordship of Jesus Christ, the purpose of the church on earth, and the miracle of salvation dramatically changed. I had encountered the holy presence of the God of Elisha, the same God who used the prophet to miraculously break the stronghold of death off the Shunnamite woman's son. My heart's desire was to be a part of the heavenly kingdom that did not discriminate because of gender, language, skin tone, physical appearance, pedigree, economic status, education, or nationality.

In America and around the world, the spirits of discrimination and segregation have contaminated many houses of worship. But what I was witnessing was a supernatural phenomenon. It was not the work of man. I witnessed the Spirit of the living God breaking down worldly barriers between people and nations as the transforming power of the Holy Ghost fell upon the people and the glory of God filled the room.

JESUS AND WOMEN DISCIPLES

MANY RELIGIOUS ORGANIZATIONS AND CHURCHES that deny godly, spiritually prepared females from holding leadership positions over the general assembly reference Apostle Paul's letter to Timothy in 1 Timothy 2:12–14 to defend their position on this highly controversial matter.

> But I suffer not a woman to teach, nor to usurp authority over a man, but to be in silence. For Adam was first formed, then Eve. And Adam was not deceived, but the woman being deceived was in the transgression.

Apostle Paul also wrote to the Corinthian church regarding some other controversial matter the disciples were grappling over. "This is the third time I am coming to you. In the mouth of two or three witnesses shall every world be established" (2 Corinthians 13:1).

He gave the church the keys to rightly dividing the word of truth. Some argue, "I can't go against the scriptures on this matter because the apostle Paul said he would not allow a woman to teach or have ecclesiastical authority over male Christians." However, when we consider Apostle Paul was indeed a chosen vessel, chosen by God to preach and teach Gentiles about the risen Savior Jesus, we know that was unheard of—a Jew teaching Gentiles! Initially, the disciples did not trust Paul because of his reputation, but his work was undeniable. They later realized Paul was no longer Saul, the tyrant and persecutor of those who followed Jesus but a yielded vessel following in the footsteps of the good shepherd, Jesus.

Perhaps we should consider Jesus's position on the subject of women speaking spiritual truths to men. We should ask the question, "If it is not appropriate for chosen female vessels to teach Christian males, why did Jesus appear to Mary Magdalene after His resurrection, delivering to her the most important message in all the world that fulfilled Old and New Testament prophesies?

> Jesus saith unto her, Mary. She turned herself, and saith unto him, Rabboni; which is to say, Master. Jesus saith unto her, Touch me not; for I am not yet ascended to my Father: but go to my brethren, and say unto them, I ascend unto my Father, and your Father; and to my God, and your God. Mary Magdalene came and told the disciples that she had seen the Lord, and that he had spoken these things unto her. (John 20:16–18)

A second witness to the mind of God on the matter of chosen women proclaiming the gospel to men in the general assembly is in Matthew 16. There were other women given messages for the male disciples regarding the resurrection of Jesus. Mary, the mother of James and Salome, arrived early in the morning the first day of the week, along with Mary Magdalene. They saw the stone was rolled away from the door of the sepulcher. They saw a young man sitting on the right side, clothed in a long white garment.

> And he said unto them, Be not affrighted: Ye seek Jesus of Nazareth, which was crucified: he is risen he is not here: behold the place where they laid him. But go your way, tell his disciples and Peter that he goeth before you into Galilee: there shall ye see him, as he said unto you. (Mark 16:6, 7)

All three books of the gospel scripture identified Mary Magdalene as a messenger sent to deliver a message to the disciples.

> Now when Jesus was risen early the first day of the week, he appeared first to Mary Magdalene, out of whom he had cast seven devils. And she went and told them that had been with him, as they mourned and wept. And they, when they had heard that he was alive, and had been seen of her, believed not.

The apostle Paul did not say it was a commandment from the Lord. Paul preferred that women not teach and for women to be silent in the church. This was his personal preference. However, in Galatians, Apostle Paul spoke about the unity of the Body of Christ, without regard to nationality, gender, or civil status. "There is neither Jew nor Greek, there is neither bond nor free, there is neither male nor female: for ye are all one in Christ Jesus" (Galatians 3:28).

Let's take a look at the word *usurp*. Apostle Paul used it in 1 Timothy 2:12– 14. The definition of *usurp* is to "take (a position of power or importance) illegally or by force." The key words are "illegally" and "by force." I've heard male leaders say, "The thing I don't like about female pastors is that they are aggressive and behave manly." Satan certainly has done a skillful job of distracting the Body of Christ from the divine purpose of Jesus establishing the church. I read an article online, published by *Charisma* magazine, on the topic of women apostles. The title of the article was "Can Women Be Apostles?" It was by Eddie Hyatt. Hyatt says,

> During the first century, while apostolic ministry was characterized by service, women freely functioned in leadership, including apostolic ministry. It was only after the church institutionalized and began to think of the apostolic in terms of office and power that women began to be excluded from leadership by men who believed their gender gave them the sole right to lead and rule. This ungodly association of the apostolic with maleness and power is still used today as a justification for excluding women from leadership in the church ... The truth is that 1 Timothy 2:11–12 was written to address a particular situation concerning Timothy and the church in Ephesus

> and was never meant to be a universal rule for all churches everywhere.

Dr. Hyatt further states,

> The choosing of 12 was never meant to be a pattern for leadership in the church. Nonetheless, the fact that Jesus chose 12 men as apostles has, throughout history, been used as the basis for excluding women from authoritative roles of leadership in the church. This line of reasoning, however, ends in absurdity if followed to its logical conclusion. Consider the fact that the 12 whom Jesus chose were not only men; they were Jewish men. Should only Jewish men be leaders in the churches? Furthermore, these 12 Jewish men were instructed by Jesus to preach only to Jews. He instructed them, "Do not go into the way of the Gentiles, and do not enter a city of the Samaritans. But go rather to the lost sheep of the house of Israel" (Matt. 15:24). If we follow this line of reasoning, we must conclude that all church leaders must be Jewish men and that they can preach only to Jewish people.

According to the Bible, men and women were created in the image of God. "So God created man in his own image, in the image of God created he him; male and female created he them" (Genesis 1:27). According to the Bible, Adam was created with dual gender. "And Adam said, 'This is now bone of my bones, and flesh of my flesh: she shall be called Woman, because she was taken out of Man'" (Genesis 2:23).

This is the mystery of "the different administration and diversities of operations." There is no dispute over the fact that men and women function differently. There are obviously anatomical differences. But that difference does not mean one or the other is superior or inferior, just different. Historically, males' and females' physical appearances were distinctly different, according to Genesis 1:27. Both males and females have God's DNA; they were created at the exact same time.

They are equal in the eyes of God. His authority supersedes human authority. The Holy Spirit is moving in the earth, stirring the hearts of women to step into their apostolic assignments now! He is saying to the male spiritual leaders, "Open the door and let My daughters come in and encourage them in the work I have called them to."

The disobedience of both Adam and Eve resulted in the gender war. Praise God for Jesus's life, death, and victorious resurrection. Jesus's obedience broke the curse over humanity. He destroyed the curse of the precedency of husbands over wives. *Merriman-Webster.com* defines *dominion* as "law: supreme authority, absolute ownership." Jesus revoked the Adamic curses when He hung on the cross, setting humanity free.

> Christ has redeemed us from the curse of the law, being made a curse for us: for it is written, everyone that hangeth on a tree. That the blessing of Abraham might come on the Gentiles through Jesus Christ; that we might receive the promise of the Spirit through faith. (Galatians 3:13, 14)

God had given Ted, my late husband, many gifts. He was an inventor. He built a prototype of a nuclear shelter that could sustain life for over thirty days without any outside intervention. He developed an air, food, and water system; placed a dove in the shelter; and sealed the door. Amazingly, at the end of thirty days, the dove was healthy and singing. When he opened the door to release the dove, it did not want to leave. That is how it is with the message of salvation. Because of the love of God and Jesus's death, burial, and resurrection, every human being is free from the curse of the law. Unfortunately, too many people do not believe it; therefore, they are damned to spend eternity in hell. God never created hell for humans but for the devil and his demons. Heaven is prepared for humans, who are created in God's image and have His breath. The curse has been abolished by the blood of the Lamb (Jesus Christ).

Believers have been redeemed and are in right standing with God in all areas of their lives. Married women in ministry who obey the word of God regarding submission to their husbands will have blessed families, marriages, and ministries. In every relationship, for the sake of achieving goals and harmony, we all must submit to one another: family, marriage, job, church, community, and so on.

> Wives, submit yourselves unto your own husbands, as unto the Lord. For the husband is the head of the wife, even as Christ is the head of the church: and he is the savior of the body. Therefore, as the church is subject unto Christ, so let the wives be to their own husbands in everything [righteous behavior]. Husbands, love your wives, even as Christ also loved the church, and gave himself for it. (Ephesians 5:22– 24)

The definition of *submit* according to *Merriam-Webster.com* is to "Yield oneself to the authority or will of another; to permit oneself to be subjected to something; to defer to or consent to abide by the opinion or authority of another." Apostle Peter says, "Likewise, ye wives, be in subjection to your own husband …" (1 Peter 3:3).

The key word in this scripture is "own." Some men, as well as women, interpret the scripture to mean every male is to dominate and rule over all females. That is not the case. There were very few males born in our immediate family. Because they were so rare, when a male child was born, the girls in the family were taught by the matriarch of the family to treat him as very special. The girls in the family were taught to wash, iron, cook, and clean the house. Boys were excused from these chores. Of course, as more males were born into the family, this practice ceased. Perhaps the older women in the family realized the importance of training males to be domesticated as well as females. Both males and females were also expected to work in the fields and in the yard.

Because of disobedience, God pronounced a severe curse upon Eve. God commanded Adam and Eve not to eat of the "tree of the knowledge of good and evil" (Genesis 2:17). Of course, she yielded to temptation and gave it to her husband, Adam, and the glory of God's presence left them; they were physically alive but spiritually dead. The tormenting spirits of guilt, shame, and condemnation oppressed and dominated their lives from that moment.

Adam and Eve's intimate relationship with their Father and Creator had been severed, and they lost their position as trustees over God's creation. They lost their authority and were driven out of paradise, the Garden of Eden, never able to regain what they had forfeited. This is the beginning of the generational curse that plagues the lives of all humans whose names are not written in the Lamb's Book of Life.

God pronounced a curse upon Adam, Eve, and the serpent. That curse fell upon all generations, beginning with Adam. According to the Bible, all humankind are descendants of Adam, the son of God. "Which was the son of Enos, which was the son of Seth, which was the son of Adam, which was the son of God" (Luke 3:38). "This is the book of the generations of Adam. In the day that God created man, in the likeness of God made he him: Male and female created he them: and blessed them, and called their name Adam, in the day when they were created" (Genesis 5:1, 2).

Humans of all ages inherited the "Adamic curse," but God had a plan in place to redeem the souls of humankind by sending his son, Jesus, to reverse the curse through the shedding of his blood and dying for the sin of the whole world. "Neither is there salvation in any other: for there is none other name under heaven given among men, whereby we must be saved" (Acts 4:12).

It is imperative that the Body of Christ realizes the magnitude of God's amazing love and compassion for every soul. This book is written to inspire women to take their rightful place in the ministry of Jesus Christ. Because of that, I will deal primarily with the curse pronounced upon Eve. Eve's name literally means "the mother of all living." From the moment Adam and Eve ate the forbidden fruit, every female born was predisposed to the curse pronounced upon Eve. "Unto the woman he said, I will greatly multiply thy sorrow and thy conception; in sorrow thou shalt bring forth children; and thy desire shall be to thy husband and he shall rule over thee" (Genesis 3:16).

Praise God for the Good News! When God sent Yeshua HaMashiach, Jesus Christ, into the world, God put in place a master plan to reverse the curse inherited by all humankind. The best-kept secret in the entire world is that God forgives sin. The apostle Paul shared this spiritual truth with the saints in Rome. "That if thou shalt confess with thy mouth the Lord Jesus, and shalt believe in thine heart that God hath raised him from the dead, thou shalt be saved" (Romans 10:9).

Anyone who confesses Jesus as Lord is no longer under the "Adamic curse" but has become a son or daughter of the God of all creation. "Beloved, now are we the sons of God, and it doth not yet appear what we shall be: but we know that, when he shall appear, we shall be like him; for we shall see him as he is" (1 John 3:2).

The children of the One True and Living God are new creatures in Christ, with new natures, making choices that produce blessings and peace instead of curses and anxiety.

Those who are spiritually mature, born-again disciples of Christ, can quickly discern the wicked spirits behind manipulation and control. God is a God of specificity. He created Adam and Eve because he desired children who are made in His image and likeness, representing Him and bringing glory to His name. God gave Adam and Eve delegated authority and dominion. "And God blessed them and said unto them. Be fruitful, and multiply and replenish the earth, and subdue it; and have dominion over the fish of the sea, and over the fowl of the air, and over every living thing that move upon the earth" (Genesis 1:27–28).

All humans, regardless of race, creed, or national origin, are made in the image and likeness of Elohim, the Creator (Genesis 1:1), and Jehovah, our Covenant Father (Genesis 2:7). God created male and female at the same time. He gave the dominion and the authority to both Adam and Eve over every living sea creature, every airborne creature, and every earthly creeping thing.

Notice the dominion and authority God gave to them did not include the dominion of humankind. When the first man and woman were created by God, there was no sin, sickness, death, or violence in the Garden of Eden. Everything God created with His word was good and very good. There was life, serenity, and harmony in the garden. Satan, the great deceiver, entered the garden and possessed the body of a serpent. He infiltrated a holy place upon the earth. Eve was created good. She did not purposely set out to disobey God. The hypnotic, seductive spirit of unbelief entered into her heart through her ear gate. The devil (Satan) came into the garden for the purpose of stealing Adam and Eve's inheritance. Satan posed a question to Eve that was designed to cause her to question God's intentions toward her and her husband by denying them full access to all the trees in the garden.

The apostle Paul, along with all humankind, wrestled with the spirit of temptation. He said, "I then find a law that when I would do good, evil is present" (Romans 7:21). The apostle James clearly describes the origin of temptation and how it overcomes an individual.

> Let no man say when he is tempted, I am tempted of God: for God cannot be tempted with evil, neither tempteth he any man: But every man is tempted, when he is drawn away of his own lust, and enticed. Then when lust hath conceived, it bringeth forth sin: and sin, when it is finished, bringeth forth death. (James 1:13–15)

From this passage, we can track the origin and progression of temptation, which results in unfavorable consequences. Every temptation can be traced back to one word, *covetousness*. Sin stems from the heart because of discontent. A question is posed to impede rational thinking followed by enticement. Covetousness impregnates the heart, and the roots of lust seize the soul, rendering it powerless. Eve was not created with the baptism of the Holy Ghost. She was never born. She was created by God and had God's breath but not His Spirit. She had nothing to restrain her. She is the perfect example of an unredeemed soul. She lacked spiritual eyesight and discernment. Eve was powerless against the cunning art of the serpent because she did not discern the serpent's subtle (crafty, cunning) nature.

Eve saw the fruit was good for food and pleasant to look at and it would make one wise. This is the nature of humankind. It is human nature to want to eat, to be attracted to what appears pleasant to look at, and to have a desire to be known as intelligent. It is human nature to go against the commandments of God. Adam and Eve had access to 99 percent of everything in the Garden of Eden but lusted after the 1 percent that belonged exclusively to God. God created Adam and Eve with "free wills." God explained the consequences if they chose to eat from the tree. "You shall surely die." Adam and Eve did not know the meaning of death. God did not have to explain its meaning because he desired voluntary obedience, not forced obedience. God gave them only one commandment to obey. "And the Lord God commanded the man, saying, Of every tree of the garden thou mayest freely eat: But of the tree of the knowledge of good and evil, thou shalt not eat of it for in the day that thou eatest thereof you shalt surely die" (Genesis 2:16, 17).

The death God referred to was spiritual death. They lost their delegated authority and dominion, the intimate relationship between them and their Father and an eternal life of pleasant productivity, abundance, and contentment. They both made a conscious decision to dishonor and challenge the authority of the Creator of the universe. Consequently, not only were Adam and Eve severely disciplined for their disobedience until the day they died, but the consequences affected every future generation. Every human born prior to the resurrection of Jesus Christ was subject to the great enemy, "the pains of death," except Enoch and Elijah. "And all the days of Enoch were three hundred sixty and five years: And Enoch walked with God: and he was not; for God took him" (Genesis 5:22–24). "And it came to pass, as they [Elijah and Elisha] still went on, and talked, that, behold, there appeared a chariot of fire, and horses of fire, and parted them both asunder; and Elijah went up by a whirlwind into heaven" (2 Kings 2:11).

The major lie and deception in the twenty-first century is that a child is born knowing and understanding the difference between good and evil, moral and immoral, righteous and unrighteousness, holy and unholy. The devil has convinced four generations that there is no need to pray to an invisible deity, and there certainly is no such thing as sin, the devil, or God and Jesus, the Son of God, and the Holy Bible is an obsolete, ancient book that is irrelevant and has no place in this highly technological society, their lives, or the lives of future generations.

How utterly deceived they are. However, there are promises of blessings, prosperity, and good success for obeying the commandments of God. It is against man's nature to do what is right and just. In the book of John, Jesus had a conversation with a man named Nicodemus. He was a religious, moral leader; we would probably call him a "good man." Unfortunately, with God, being "good" is not a ticket to heaven. Nicodemus was in danger of not seeing the kingdom of God because he was not born again. Jesus shared with this "good" religious leader an important truth unknown by the chief priests and rabbis. "Jesus answered and said unto him Verily, verily, I say unto thee, Except a man be born again, he cannot see the kingdom of God" (John 3:3).

Jesus was emphasizing the importance of the new birth. Until a person is born again of the spirit and of the water, the "Adamic" nature (rebelliousness and disobedience) will always challenge the "will and commandments of God." Paul identified this as the "law of disobedience," known as lust, that exists in the heart of every human born on the earth.

There are three major categories for temptation: the lust of the flesh, the lust of the eye, and the pride of life. After Jesus was baptized, the Spirit drove Him into the wilderness to be tempted of the devil for forty days and nights. During that time, the devil tried over and over to entice and lure Jesus into falling down and worshipping him. Praise God, Jesus resisted the devil and began His ministry with power and authority (Matthew 4:1–17).

Darkness and wickedness entered the world through disobedience. But righteousness and peace came through Jesus Christ. His sinless life, agonizing death, humble burial, and victorious resurrection restored the broken relationship between humankind and God. The delegated authority and dominion over the fish of the seas, the birds of the air, and every earthly creeping thing was restored and expanded because of Jesus's resurrection to include authority over all principalities, every power, and every demonic spirit by appropriating the name of Jesus Christ. "Behold I give unto you power to tread on serpents and scorpions, and over all the power of the enemy: and nothing shall by any means hurt you" (Luke 10:19).

God did not exclude Eve when he pronounced the authority and power. She was equal with Adam in every sense. The subtle devil has once again deceived clergymen for thousands of years by questioning God's intentions, authority, and Word.

In these end times, the devil is saying to the church, "Surely God does not use females in the apostolic ministry; let them follow you and support you financially, but do not accept them as colaborers in ministry. Remember it was a woman who was deceived by the devil." Satan, the "chief strategist," has been successful in keeping the Body of Christ from producing the number of disciples it could have, because the church has failed to recognize the deception that crept into the church. Jesus never placed a disclaimer on the Great Commission regarding who was or was not permitted to go into all the world and preach and teach the gospel. We are all called to work the works of God. Jesus said, "Verily, verily, I say unto you; He that believeth on me, the works that I do shall he do also; and greater works than these shall he do because I go unto my Father" (John 14:12).

Whether you are male or female reading this book, God's will for you is that you discover and fulfill your ordained purpose. You have been born to do something specific while on the earth that manifests God's love for humanity. Lying demons and devils are in the world to stop the liberating message of salvation from reaching people who have not heard the good news that their sins are forgiven because Jesus redeemed them from the curse of the law when he died on the cross and rose with all power and dominion. If all believers modeled themselves after the Savior by obeying the Word of God and allowing the Holy Spirit to abide in them, the church of Jesus Christ would once again turn the world upside down.

It will take supernatural signs, wonders, and miracles to capture the hearts and minds of the people today and those born in future generations. The Body of Christ can only complete the Great Commission of Jesus Christ by the power and counsel of the Holy Ghost.

Jesus came preforming miracles because the social climate when He was on earth was similar to our present world's. People were doing what was right in their own eyes, and there was considerable unbelief, self-righteousness, religious oppression, poverty, disease, infirmity, and plague. Today, the spirit of unbelief and sin is widespread in America more than at any other time in history. We are witnessing the consequences of forsaking the commandments of God and failing to teach them to the children. Because of social media, inventions, illusions, and mysticism, the church must rely on the spirit of truth coming from heaven to open the spiritual eyes of the Body of Christ to discern truth from lies, good from evil, and angels of light from the angels of darkness.

I believe God will once again release His supernatural power upon the Body of Christ, for miracles, signs, and wonders. It will take the same power and the same anointing Jesus had to reach the hearts and minds of this end time generation with the message of salvation through Jesus Christ.

GOD'S SPIRIT

WOMEN IN THE BODY OF Christ, get ready. Don't throw up your hands, go home, and sit down or silently sit passively in the pews of the churches. *Now is your time.* Your time of enduring tremendous oppression, persecution, discrimination, public humiliation, abandonment, sexual harassment, financial abuse, and character assassination is over! It is harvesttime, and the Spirit of God is being poured out. God spoke through His servant Joel and said, "Be glad then ye children of Zion, and rejoice in the Lord your God: for he hath given you the former rain moderately, and he will cause to come down for you the rain, the former rain, and the latter rain in the first month" (Joel 2:23).

This particular scripture denotes blessings upon God's people. Moderate rain means just the right amount, not too much or too little. Rain will fall from heaven. That is the lifeline and sustenance for those who are obedient. Once the people of God are refreshed, God does even more.

> And it shall come to pass afterward, that I will pour out my spirit upon all flesh; and your sons and your daughters shall prophesy, your old men shall dream dreams, your young men shall see vision: And also upon the servants and upon the handmaids in those days will I pour out my spirit. (Joel 2:28–29)

Often, women in the church are subjected to spiritual abuse resulting in becoming a casualty in a spiritual war and, too often, do not recover. God is calling for more apostolic women who will counsel these women from the scriptures, patiently listening and praying for them. Christian women with apostolic callings are under tremendous pressure from their sisters in Christ because these women do not understand the apostolic call and associate this calling with maleness. Therefore, the apostolic woman is looked upon with suspicion. Women with an apostolic calling often experience rejection by both genders in the Body of Christ. But it becomes even more spiritually challenging when women in the church withdraw from them or resent them, failing to realize by encouraging the apostolic women to fulfill their calling, it raises the status of all women, by weakening preconceived ideas about the equality of women with men in the eyes of God. Many apostolic women are wives, mothers, and grandmothers who understand a successful ministry begins with a healthy home. They are faithful, devoted wives to their husbands and loving, nurturing mothers to their children. Although they are feminine and appreciate beautiful things, they are modest and not obsessed with the things of this world but passionate about soul winning and imparting spiritual truths that have the power to transform lives.

However, the apostolic calling is not a glamorous social calling but one that is consecrated. The Holy Spirit directs the steps of the apostolic woman. He leads and guides her by inspiration and through the Holy Scriptures. He counsels her and provides revelation knowledge concerning every aspect of her life and ministry. Nothing compares to or is so glorious as meditating on the Word and in fellowship with her heavenly Father. Her disciplined spiritual lifestyle results in a close, intimate relationship with God and His Son, Jesus Christ. The apostolic woman lives, moves, and breathes in anticipation of the next assignment. Her greatest pleasure is witnessing the spiritual growth of her family members and those she ministers to. She relies on the comfort and guidance of the Holy Spirit and listens intently for divine instructions. She has spiritual eyesight, watching for opportunities to emulate her Savior and do the will of her Father in heaven by serving humanity, laying hands on the sick that they may recover, casting out devils, setting captives free from demonic influences, raising the dead, and preaching and teaching repentance, the second coming of Jesus Christ, end-time prophecy, and the glorious kingdom of God.

The apostolic woman is a visionary, establishing churches, Bible schools, prayer centers, healing homes, orphanages, day schools, counseling centers, shelters, and deliverance centers. Her passion is evangelizing. She looks for opportunities to impart the evangelistic anointing to others for the purpose of advancing the kingdom of God and to share biblical truths with followers of Christ, freeing them from binding spirits of shame, guilt, and condemnation in order that they may also become "fishers of men." Under the directions of the Holy Spirit, she may establish schools of ministry to train, equip, and commission laborers to go into the fields of the world to harvest souls. The apostolic woman speaks to and stirs up dormant spiritual gifts in believers. The Holy Ghost endows her with supernatural power and a compelling desire to stay in the perfect will of God and to follow in the footsteps of Jesus and remain faithful and obedient to finish the course that is set before her while on earth.

Precious daughter of God there is a call from your Heavenly Father to shake off the chains that have held you captive. Jesus broke your chains at Calvary when He, who was sinless, suffered, bled, and died on a Roman cross. He was quickened by the Spirit of God after three days in the grave and defeated Satan and death by walking out of the tomb with an immortal body possessing all power and all authority in heaven and in earth.

Before Jesus's death and resurrection, He proclaimed his mission for coming to earth in Luke 4:18: "I came to preach deliverance to the captives ... to set at liberty those that are bound."

There is a clarion call for apostolic women all over the world to share the message of complete liberty in Christ. God loves men and women equally. He created males and females at the same time, and His plan is for them to step into their ordained spiritual callings and to keep their focus on the work at hand, *souls, souls, souls*!

I believe we are the end-time generation that will experience the Harpazo, "catching away," of the believers of Jesus Christ. The meaning is derived from the Latin word *rapturo* meaning "caught up." The rapture of the saints is an amazing revelation intended to instill hope in believers enduring persecution. The premier verses concerning the doctrine of the rapture are 1 Thessalonians 4:14–18.

The very fact we are witnessing the fulfillment of the events Jesus foretold in Matthew 24 is an indicator that the end of time is rapidly approaching. Therefore, He is calling every soldier of Christ to active duty in order to fulfill the Great Commission and to be courageous and bold enough to proclaim, "I am an unashamed Christian. A true disciple of Jesus Christ, Son of the Living God. The devil does not have the power or authority to muzzle me or to silence me. Jesus has all power and all authority. Therefore, I am under His authority and speak and act in the name of Jesus Christ."

"And Jesus came and spake unto them, saying, All power is given unto me in heaven and in earth" (Matthew 28:18).

Jesus has given believers the authority to use His name to bind (restrict) or loose (free) things on earth, and they shall be bound or loosed in heaven. Even more incredible is when believers ask anything in Jesus's name, He does it, and the Father is glorified.

Jesus said, "And whatsoever ye shall ask in my name, that will I do, that the Father may be glorified in the Son. If ye shall ask any thing in my name, I will do" (John 14:13).

Jesus gives believers *dunamis* power (miraculous physical power, force, might, ability, efficacy, energy) to produce the intended results. It is unexplainable and supernatural. He gives us the ability to do things we could never accomplish with our human abilities, worldly knowledge, or physical strength.

"Behold, I give unto you power to tread on serpents and scorpions, and over all the power of the enemy: and nothing shall by any means hurt you" (Luke 10:19).

It is imperative that believers understand that the events Jesus foretold in Matthew 24 will definitely take place in Israel. When we see prophecies fulfilled by studying the scriptures and listening to the news or reading newspapers, we know it will not be long before Jesus Christ returns for the purpose of removing Christians from this world, to spare them from the wrath to come, just like He protected the Israelites from the judgment that came upon Egypt (Deuteronomy 7:14; 12:36).

"And as he [Jesus] sat upon the mount of Olives, the disciples came unto him privately, saying, Tell us, when shall these things be? And what shall be the sign of thy coming, and of the end of the world?" (Matthew 24:3).

In the same chapter of Matthew, Jesus clearly describes the events that will take place in the end times. One very significant sign pointing to the signs of His coming and the end of the world was in verse 14: "And this gospel of the kingdom shall be preached in the world for a witness unto all nations; and then shall the end come."

God released in our generation modes of transportation and technology that were unknown to previous generations. Because of these God-inspired inventions, we have done greater works than Jesus and the New Testament Church to disseminate the gospel message.

On December 23, 2016, the United Nations Council voted fourteen to zero for Israelis to halt their settlement efforts. This action by the UNSC was not against the Israelites but against God. The land belongs to God. Scripture declares the absolute ownership of the Middle East and the whole world in Psalm 24:1, "The earth is the Lord's and the fullness thereof; the world, and they that dwell therein." Because God owns Israel, He has the authority to give it to whomever He wishes. He chose to give it to Abram. There are hundreds of scriptures regarding the sanctity of the land of Israel and His seed.

> And the Lord said unto Abram, after that Lot was separated from him. "Lift up now thine eyes, and look from the place where thou art northward, and southward, and eastward, and westward: For all the land which thou seest, to thee will I give it, and to thy seed forever." (Genesis 13:14–15)

Regardless of the pressure placed upon the Israelites, giving up land and halting the settlement is a violation of God's commandments, placing them under the judgment of God. God commanded Israel to never sell the land. "The land shall not be sold for ever; for the land is mine; for ye are strangers and sojourners with me" (Leviticus 25:23).

The United Nations Security Council's compulsion of the Israelis to comply with their demands clearly points to some troubling days ahead in the Middle East, to the extent it just could usher in the fulfillment of the entire chapter of Matthew 24. Jesus said, "And except those days should be shortened, there should no flesh be saved: but for the elect's sake those days shall be shortened" (Matthew 24:22).

This is why it is imperative that every disciple of Christ know the time and season we are living in. God is calling for the Body of Christ to become one in the spirit and to seek His counsel for the wisdom to reach more souls, to teach people everywhere about the God of Israel and Jesus Christ, the Savior of the world, that they may be ready when the trump of God sounds, wakening those who are asleep in the Lord and summoning those who are alive to meet Jesus in the air to attend the Lamb's marriage supper.

We are living in critical times. Every believer in Jesus Christ is urgently needed now! The Holy Spirit is drafting all whose names are written in the Lamb's book of life to service in the army of the Lord. I worked in a penal institution, and whenever there was a threat of takeover of the institution by the prisoners or a prisoner escaped, every peace officer was called to protect the safety of the community and the life of every person in the institution. Satan is determined to destroy the very fabric of our society, specifically the traditional family, procreation, and human life. Church, wake up! Get up! Reap the harvest! The harvest is ripe and waiting for the harvesters.

MIDNIGHT CRY

JESUS SAID, "WATCH THEREFORE: FOR ye know neither the day nor the hour wherein the Son of man cometh" (Matthew 25:13). "Therefore be ye also ready for in such an hour as ye think not the Son of man cometh" (Matthew 24:44).

Sisters, brothers, it is time for the corporate Body of Christ to be single minded and focused on one thing, fulfilling the Great Commission. Jesus commanded, "But seek ye first the Kingdom of God, and His righteousness; and all these things shall be added unto you" (Matthew 6:33). Jesus died for the souls of every boy, girl, man, and woman. He shed His precious blood and took away the sin of every soul who would ever live on this earth and has given them everlasting life. The quandary is that they don't know Jesus's shed blood washed their sin away forever. That is why Jesus said, "Go ye into all the world, and preach the gospel to every creature" (Mark 16:15).

The New Testament church taught and preached what Jesus taught and preached. They duplicated His works by delivering the bound, setting captives free, healing the sick, and declaring the kingdom of God and the gospel of Jesus Christ. The end-time church is commissioned to stay the course by studying and obeying the teachings of Jesus and continuing the work of the New Testament church.

The church Jesus Christ established on the earth was to remain until Christ returns. The church's responsibility is to prepare the world for Jesus's return by sharing the gospel, teaching believers scriptures, becoming soulwinners, looking for Jesus to return, and being ready to govern with Jesus Christ as kings and priests during His thousand-year reign on the earth.

> And they sung a new song, saying, Thou art worthy to take the book, and to open the seals thereof: for thou wast slain, and hast redeemed us to God by the blood out of every kindred, and tongue, and people, and nation; And hast made us unto our God kings and priests: and we shall reign on the earth. (Revelation 5:9, 10)

Therefore, evangelism and schools of ministry should be the primary function of the church—teaching every man, woman, boy, and girl scriptures from Genesis to Revelation in preparation for the end of the age. "And when all things shall be subdued unto him, then shall the Son also himself be subject unto him that put all things under him, that God may be all in all" (1 Corinthians 15:28).

I know some of you are saying, "I don't understand how I can be a part of God's kingdom now." Well, Jesus said we were not of this world. He prayed for everyone who would become His disciple. "I pray not that thou should take them out of the world, but that thou shouldest keep them from the evil. They are not of the world, even as I am not of the world" (John 17:15, 16).

When we accept Jesus as our Savior, we are supernaturally changed. We receive a new nature. The apostle Paul describes the manifestation of the new nature. He said, "Therefore, if any man be in Christ, he is a new creature: old things are passed away; behold all things are become new" (1 Corinthians 5:17).

The beloved apostle John further addresses the transformation that takes place when we receive Christ.

> And this is the record, that God hath given to us eternal life, and this life is in his Son. He that hath the Son hath life; and he that hath not the Son of God hath not life. These things have I written unto you that believe on the name of the Son of God; that ye may know that ye have eternal life, and that ye may believe on the name of the Son of God. (1 John 5:11–13)

According to the World Population Clock, the current world population is 7.6 billion as of December 2017.[2] Out of the 7.6 billion humans living, 2.18 billion are Christians. In the United States, Christians declined from more than three-quarters of the population in 2010 and are expected to decline to two-thirds in 2050, and Judaism will no longer be the largest non-Christian religion. Muslims will be more numerous in the United States than people who identify as Jewish, on the basis of religion.[3]

Perhaps looking at when humanity began will serve to provide insight into the number of years Jesus has been preparing for our arrival to His heavenly kingdom and the nearness of His return and the "catching away" of His disciples. God, with His infinite wisdom, concealed the day and hour when He will send Jesus to summon believers from every nation to the marriage supper of the lamb. Neither Jesus, the angels, Satan, nor any human knows when the trump of God will sound. One sign of false teachers and prophets is claiming to know the day and hour of Jesus's return.

> But of that day and hour knoweth no man, no, not the angels of heaven, but my Father only. But as the days of Noe were, so shall also the coming of the Son of man be. For as in the days that were before the flood they were eating and drinking, marrying and giving in marriage, until the day that Noe entered into the ark, and knew not until the flood came, and took them all away; do shall also the coming of the Son of man be. (Matthew 24:36–39)

The Bible tells us in John 3:16 that God loves the world. It is not His will that any perish; that is the purpose for Jesus coming to earth—that none die in their sins. The sacred Holy Scriptures were written and remain today to lead people to the only true and living God in order that they may know their origin and their creator. God wants people to know this world is not their home. It is not their final destination but only a journey. Although no one but God knows when He will send Jesus to gather His people, Jesus left on record through scriptures in Matthew 24 specific signs to watch for that point to the season of His return and the events leading to the end of the world. Jesus instructed his disciples to watch—and not only to watch but to go and spread the news that Jesus is coming again to the whole world.

Today, we are living in a world where good is called bad and right is considered wrong. Even people going to church are saying, "I don't see anything wrong with what is going on in the world. People have a right to their own opinion and to do what they think is right for them." This attitude is the reason our world is in the shape it is today. Just as children need guidance from parents, the children of God need guidance from the Bible. Jesus said, "And except those days should be shortened, there should no flesh be saved; but for the elect's sake these days shall be shortened" (Matthew 24:22).

Apostle Paul provides the framework for keeping unity and peace in the Body of Christ.

> I therefore, the prisoner of the Lord, beseech you that ye walk worthy of the vocation wherewith ye are called, With all lowliness and meekness, with long suffering, forbearing one another in love; Endeavoring to keep the unity of the Spirit in the bond of peace. (Ephesians 4:1–3)

It is doubtful that he was addressing only men while in Ephesus. He was speaking to the general assembly, and this passage of scripture clearly outlines how those who are called by God as leaders in the Lord's church are to walk humbly before God and one another, for the sake of peace in our churches. Oh, how it must grieve our heavenly Father to see His children plotting to set traps for one another and standing in the way of each other's work. Listen to the prayer of our Lord. "And now I am no more in the world, and I come to thee. Holy Father keep through thine own name those whom thou hast given me, that they may be one, as we are" (John 17:11).

> Ephesians 4:4-6 reveals Paul's heart cry for oneness in the Body of Christ. There is one body, and one Spirit, even as ye are called in one hope of your calling; One Lord,

> one faith, one baptism One God and Father of all, who is above all, and through all, and in you all.

The time of sorrow Jesus spoke about in Matthew 24:8 is now. The church has been distracted. There should never have been a debate about ministry callings in the Body of Christ. Love within the Body of Christ will attract the people in the world to Jesus Christ. Jesus Christ commands us to love one another.

"A new commandment I give unto you, That ye love one another, as I have loved you, that ye also love one another. By this shall all men know that ye are my disciples, if ye have love one to another" (John 13:34, 35).

Love is not an option. Love for God and one another are the elements that will convince the world that Jesus is who He claimed to be, Savior, Redeemer, because our lives will be a reflection of His.

SILENCE

MALACHI, THE LAST BOOK OF the Old Testament, describes how Israel's lack of love, reverence, and fear of God, resulted in four hundred years of silence. During those dark years, the prophet's voice was silent, and God was not communicating with humankind. You can't help but wonder, How did they get into such a devastating state where their Creator had nothing to say to them?

Today's spiritual climate is similar to when the Prophet Malachi lived. God spoke through him about His severe displeasure with Israel. American and the rest of the world appear to be emulating the same sinful behavior as Israel. God saw their prideful, wicked hearts and their arrogant behavior, and it vexed His spirit, resulting in God pronouncing a perpetual judgment upon them.

> Whereas Edom saith, We are impoverished, but we will return and build the desolate places; thus saith the Lord of host, They shall build, but I will throw down; and they shall call them the border of wickedness, and The people against whom the Lord hath indignation forever. (Malachi 1:4)

America and the nations of the world are experiencing unprecedented death and destruction due to war, storms, deadly diseases, famine, and plagues. The only hope for the world is for the spiritual leaders to prostrate themselves before God by repenting for their sins, seeking restoration of their souls, and surrendering themselves to the master. God said He will heal the land and withdraw the judgment upon the earth. When those we lead observe our holy lifestyles, they will become holy; they will pray and consecrate themselves to God. Second Chronicles 7:14 tells us what God will do in response to those who are called by His name: "If my people, which are called by my name, shall humble themselves, and pray, and seek my face, and turn from their wicked ways; then will I hear from heaven, and will forgive their sin, and will heal their land."

He will heal our land. Everyone will be blessed because the ministers of the Lord are walking in truth and righteousness. They are walking in obedience to the commandments and statutes of God. God is merciful and just and rewards righteousness but disciplines the disobedient. Why? Because He truly loves His children.

The only hope for future generations throughout the world is a return to God and for parents to train up their children according to the Bible by teaching them to govern their lives according to scripture. Children need instructions in righteousness. The Ten Commandments God wrote with His own hand; if followed, they would reduce the number of violent crimes committed around the world. If the Holy Bible once again became the fundamental textbook in our schools and universities, Roe v. Wade would be overturned; the covenant of marriage would be honored, reducing divorce rates and broken homes; marriage between a male and female would once again be restored; integrity and concern for the welfare of consumers would be restored to merchants and farmers; homelessness, mental illness, alcoholism, and substance abuse would decrease; children would honor their parents; adult children would love and care for their aging parents; and greed for money would no longer override the consciences of politicians, and they would legislate based upon the Holy Word of God.

Malachi, the last book of the Old Testament, is very somber. The neglect and failure of the priest to teach the people the commandments of God was the direct result of the moral decline of the people.

Malachi 2:7–10, 14–16 says,

> For the priest's lips should keep knowledge, and they should seek the law at his mouth: for he is the messenger of the Lord of hosts. But ye are departed out of the way; ye have caused many to stumble at the law; ye have corrupted the covenant of Levi, saith the Lord of host. Therefore,

> have I also made you contemptible and base before all the people according as ye have not kept my ways but have been partial in the law. Have we not all one father? Hath not one God created us? Why do we deal treacherously every man against his brother, by profaning the covenant of our father?
>
> Yet ye say, Wherefore: Because the Lord hath been witness between thee and the wife of thy youth, against when thou hast dealt treacherously: yet is she thy companion, and the wife of thy covenant ... Therefore take heed to your spirit, and let none deal treacherously against thy wife. For the Lord, the God of Israel, saith that he hateth putting away: for one covereth violence with his garment, saith the Lord of hosts: therefore take heed to your spirit that ye deal not treacherously. Ye have wearied the Lord with your words. Yet ye say, Wherein have we wearied him? When ye say, Every one that doeth evil is good in the sight of the Lord, and he delighteth in them; or, Where is the God of judgment?

Several years ago, I met a Christian woman who told me her church never studied the Old Testament because it was not relevant for today. When she said that, I thought about the scripture where God said, "My people are destroyed for lack of knowledge: because thou hast rejected knowledge, I will also reject thee, that thou shalt be no priest to me: seeing thou hast forgotten the law of thy God, I will also forget thy children" (Hosea 4:6).

The message of "grace" without the knowledge of the commandments and statutes of God is like a bath without water. Jesus said, "Think not that I am come to destroy the law, or the prophets: I am not come to destroy, but to fulfil" (Matthew 5:17).

No wonder our society is in such a deplorable condition. The people are doing what is right in their own eyes because spiritual leaders are failing to teach the full counsel of God, as written in the Holy Bible.

Recurrently, Israel forgot the LORD and how He supernaturally delivered and sustained them and began to worship idol gods like the heathen nations around them. They left YHWH, the great "I Am That I Am" and voluntarily ran into the arms of the devil, the thief, killer, and destroyer.

Yet the LORD's arms were stretched out toward Israel, just as the arms of Jesus are stretched out to America and the rest of the world. He is patiently waiting and looking for His wayward laborers and fishermen to return to their fields and boats. The harvest is ripe, and the fish are plentiful.

EXONERATED

THE FIRST BOOK OF THE New Testament began with these words, "The genealogy of Jesus Christ, the son of David, the son of Abraham" (Matthew 1:1). I find amazing the unimaginable ways God expresses forgiveness and restoration. Eve was enticed by the subtle serpent. The serpent was a beast who lived in the garden and Eve was undoubtably familiar with him. After all, Adam named him. It is doubtful Adam and Eve fully understood the ramifications of disobeying God's commandment, which serves as a reminder that disobedience is a serious sin. When God says, "Thou shalt not!" take Him at His word, and don't do it. God is not required to tell us why He is saying, "Thou shalt not!" God is the creator. We are His creation and exist because He willed us to exist. Do we dare use His breath of life to question God's authority?

Eve's name means "mother of all living" (Genesis 3:20). What a high position God placed her in. Disobedience resulted in Eve's forfeiting her position as the mother of all life. Scripture says she gave the forbidden fruit to Adam, and he ate as well. A curse was pronounced upon her. She was banished from the garden. She suffered heartache and witnessed the conflict between her sons, resulting in the death of one and eternal separation from the other. Her actions resulted in a curse pronounced upon her. Because she was female, it has been taught and believed by the church that every female is cursed, by virtue of the fact she is born female. That is not true from what I've read in the Bible regarding God's relationship with females. Those who faithfully worshipped God were blessed and favored by God. The same is true of men who were faithful to worship God. This belief about females being cursed has been used by men to exclude women from leadership positions in the church; in fact, when Adam and Eve disobeyed God's commandment, it altered the future of all creation, not just humans. Adam and Eve had to suffer the consequences of their disobedience. They were disciplined for their actions. The ground was cursed, and Adam had to toil and work hard to sustain their life. Eve would experience great pain when conceiving and suffer great pains during childbirth; her relationship would no longer be harmonious, and Adam would have dominion over her.

The consequences of Adam and Eve's failure to obey God's commandment not to eat of the tree of the knowledge of good and evil resulted in the catastrophic climax to immortality for all creation. Adam and Eve were to live forever. God's plan for them did not include the ravaging effects of aging. Animals, birds, sea creatures, grass, flowers, and all living things were to live forever in their beautiful, perfect state.

"Unto the woman he (God) said, I will greatly multiply thy sorrow and thy conception; in sorrow thou shalt bring forth children; and thy desire shall be to thy husband, and he shall rule over thee" (Genesis 2:16). In my Bible, there is a reference scripture of 1 Timothy 2:12, where Apostle Paul said, "But I suffer not a woman to teach, nor usurp authority over the man, but to be silent."

One must ask the question, if the curse pronounced upon Eve was transferred to all females, to bear children in pain and to be dominated by their husbands, what about the woman who never bore children or married? If all females were cursed, why would God choose a cursed female to conceive His Son? When God chose Mary of Nazareth to conceive in her womb Jesus, heaven and earth witnessed the loving, merciful character of God, revealing God looks on the individual character of each woman and does not punish or judge her by another's disobedience. It is true; Eve was sentenced to a life of heartache, pain, and suffering. Women are taught by their mothers that being female is just a suffering life. Mary was a young girl from a small town. She was from the lineage of Adam and Eve, just as every human is, yet God called her blessed even before she conceived the Son of God.

When God chose a female to carry, protect, and nurture the "Savior of the World," He was revealing His righteous judgment and love for females.

> In the sixth month, the angel Gavri'el [Gabriel] was sent by God to a city in the Galil [Galilee] called Natzeret [Nazareth], to a virgin engaged to a man named Yosef [Joseph] of the house of David; the virgin's name was Miryam [Mary]. Approaching her, the angel said, "Shalom [Peace], favored lady! Adonai is with you!" She was deeply troubled by his words and wondered what kind of greeting this might be, The angel said to her, "Don't be afraid, Miryam, for you have found favor with God. Look! You will become pregnant, you will give birth to a son, and you are to name him Yeshus [Jesus]. He will be great, he will be called Son of Ha'Elyon [The Most High], Adonai [Master, Lord, Lord], God, will give him the throne of his forefather David; and he will rule the House of Ya'akov [Jacob] forever—there will be no end to his Kingdom." "How can this be," asked Miryam of the angel "since I am a virgin?" The angel answered her, "The Ruach HaKodesh [Holy Ghost, Holy Spirit] will come over you, the power of Ha'Elyon will cover you. Therefore the holy child born to you will be called the Son of God." (Luke 1:26–35)

To fully understand the significance of this act of amazing love and grace is to experience restoration and liberation from all emotional and mental bondages. God could have created Jesus as an adult like Adam and Eve. They had no mother. They were never infants, toddlers, or adolescents. Adam and Eve did not go through the human growth developmental stages. But God chose to send Jesus into the world as an embryo experiencing every stage of development in order that we may know that Jesus truly understands everything we go through as humans, and we can follow in His footsteps and resist temptation and overcome satanic influences when we surrender our lives and wills to God.

"For we have not an high priest which cannot be touched with the feelings of our infirmities; but was in all points tempted like as we are, yet without sin" (Hebrew 4:15).

God chose Mary of Nazareth, who was from a priestly lineage, to be the vessel he would use for this world-changing event. The Son of God would draw His nourishment from her and rest in her gentle arms. Mary of Nazareth was granted the highest-ranking spiritual leadership position, as the mother of Jesus, Son of God. Mary was entrusted with the Son of God, who would die for the sin of the whole world and change the course of history.

Mary was literally responsible for lovingly nourishing and protecting Emmanuel (God with us) in the womb and reverently raised Him knowing He was Israel's promised Messiah. Mary's willingness to submit to this challenging but honorable role is expressed in her response to the messenger angel Gabriel.

> And Mary said, "My soul doth magnify the Lord, And my spirit hath rejoiced in God my Savior. For he hath regarded the low estate of his handmaiden: for, behold from henceforth all generations shall call me blessed. For he that is mighty hath done to me great things; and holy is his name. And his mercy is on them that fear him from generation to generation. He hath shewed strength with his arm; he hast scattered the proud in the imagination of their hearts. He hast put down the mighty from their seats, and exalted them of low degree. He hast filled the hungry with good things; and the rich he hath sent empty away. He hath holpen his servant Israel, in remembrance of his mercy; As he spake to our fathers, to Abraham, and to his seed for ever." (Luke 1:46–55)

VESSELS OF GOD

IN THE BOOK OF MATTHEW, there are two notable women listed in the genealogy of Jesus: Ruth, the Moabite, the grandmother of King David, and Mary, the mother of Jesus Christ, the Son of God. This is significant because the entry of Jesus into the world brought liberation to females. God gave life to millions of females throughout the ages who were born for a specific purpose related to the sustainability of the nation of Israel and the advancement of the kingdom of God. However, because of men and many women considering females as inferior, these women never fulfilled their ordained purpose during their lifetimes.

The ministry of Jesus Christ eradicated the tradition prohibiting women from studying the law and prophets. The Spirit of God divinely guided the hands of the scribe in the writing of the book of Matthew to include the names of Ruth and Mary. God chose Ruth, a Gentile who worshipped the God of Abraham, Isaac, and Jacob and married a wealthy Hebrew man named Boaz. She is the mother of Jesse, the father of David, who was the anointed king of Israel and a man after God's own heart. God favored Mary of Nazareth with the honor of giving birth to the "Lamb of God," who would die for the sins of the world. She mothered the child who would restore humans back to their creator, "I Am, That I Am, YHVH."

It's unimaginable to think about, but what if Ruth had been denied entry to Bethlehem because she was not an Israelite? David, the anointed prophet and king, would not have been born. What if Mary, an unmarried girl, had been stoned when the priest discovered she was pregnant? The Messiah would have never lived to manifest to the world the compassionate, loving character of our heavenly Father to forgive sin. Be that as it may, nothing or no one could alter God's divine blueprints for the preservation of Israel and redemption of human souls. God's desire is for humans to live blessed lives upon the earth and, at the fulfillment of all things, spend eternity with Him, Jesus, and the saints of the ages in the New Jerusalem.

The ministry of Jesus literally revolutionized the lives of females. His presence in the world dramatically changed their destiny. He set females free from the bondage of oppression and spiritual illiteracy.

Jesus delivered Mary Magdalene from seven tormenting devils. After she was set free, she expressed her gratitude by totally surrendering her life as a devoted, faithful, supporting disciple of Jesus Christ. "And certain women, which had been healed of evil spirits and infirmities, Mary called Magdalene, out of whom went seven devils ..." (Luke 8:2).

She is mentioned fourteen times in the gospels, and from the references of her, we can see clearly what she did and how she did it. Mary Magdalene's name heads the list when mentioned in scripture along with other women. In the five times where she is mentioned alone, the connection is with the death and resurrection of Christ.

"Now when Jesus was risen early the first day of the week, he appeared first to Mary Magdalene, out of whom he had cast seven devils" (Mark 16:9).

> The first day of the week cometh Mary Magdalene early, when it was yet dark, unto the sepulchre, and seeth the stone taken away from the sepulcher. But Mary stood without at the sepulcher weeping: and as she wept, she stooped down, and looked into the sepulcher. Jesus said unto her, Mary. She turned herself, and saith unto him, Rabboni, which is to say, Master. Mary Magdalene came and told the disciples that she had seen the Lord, and that he had spoken these things unto her. (John 20:1, 11, 16, 18)

In one instance, Mary Magdalene's name comes after Mary, the mother of Jesus, and Mary, the aunt of Jesus. She stood close by the cross with these grieving family members.

"Now there stood by the cross of Jesus his mother, and his mother's sister, Mary the wife of Cleophas, and Mary Magdalene" (John 19:25). No woman, however, superseded Mary Magdalene's level of involvement in the active ministry of Jesus Christ and her utter devotion to proclaiming the message that Jesus was indeed the promised Messiah. Mary Magdalene's name appears more in scripture than any of the male disciples'. This is an obvious indication of the vast wealth of knowledge she acquired from the Messiah. A number of women disciples traveled with Jesus: Mary Magdalene; Joanna, the wife of Herod's steward Chuza; and Susanna (Luke 8:1–3).

The women who accompanied Jesus and the twelve men journeyed from one town and village to another, preaching and proclaiming the good news of the Messiah and His teachings. We know from the Gospel of Matthew that Jesus blessed five loaves and two fishes and fed five thousand men, besides women and children. Women who followed Jesus received the same teachings as the male disciples, and women disciples received the same commission as their male counterparts. Unfortunately, we have not had access to documentation regarding their ministries, and only a few women are named in the four gospels.

"And they that had eaten were about five thousand men, beside women and children" (Matthew 14:21).

There are several scriptures describing Jesus's encounter with women, and nothing reveals the slightest hint of partiality. He treated men and women equally. When Jesus stood in the temple, He read from Isaiah 61 and declared the scripture was fulfilled, which meant the captives were set free. This unpopular decree was ensuring equitable treatment for everyone who believes the gospel message. The Bible has survived despite every effort of man to destroy it because it is absolute truth, the Living Word of Almighty God, recorded for the welfare of humanity. Apostle Paul reminded the church in Rome that Jesus Christ pleased not Himself. As the followers of Christ, neither should we.

"Let every one of us please his neighbor for his good to edification. For whatsoever things were written aforetime were written for our learning, that we through patience and comfort of the scriptures might have hope" (Romans 15:2, 4).

Jesus didn't deny Mary access to His teachings. He welcomed her and embraced her eagerness to learn about the kingdom of God. Martha, Mary's sister, complained to Jesus about Mary not assisting with the preparation of the meal. Jesus responded in a way that reaffirms His position of "no schisms in the Body of Christ" when it comes to females having access to the Word of God, as well as males. Jesus said, "But one thing is needful, and Mary hath chosen that good part, which shall not be taken away from her" (Luke 10:42).

After examining scriptures regarding the interaction between Jesus and the women who followed Him, there should be no question about the inclusion of women to fight in this spiritual battle. Male and female disciples are called to snatch hell-bound souls out of the hands of the devil. In this very dark, wicked, sin-laden world, every disciple is needed. Regardless of age, gender, or disability, Jesus is calling His disciples to the front line to proclaim the gospel that Jesus set the whole world free from the curse of sin. All they have to do is believe the message and receive their freedom. Apostle John, the beloved disciple, accompanied Jesus and recorded what he heard and witnessed while traveling with Him. "The next day John [the Baptist] seeth Jesus coming unto him, and saith, 'Behold the Lamb of God, which taketh away the sin of the world'" (John 1:29).

Our Lord commended Mary for choosing the good part and decreed it shall not be taken away from her. Jesus spent personal time teaching Mary. It is extremely doubtful that Mary failed to teach others what Jesus had taught her or do what she saw Him do as He ministered to the people.

Jesus was only twelve years old when He told His mother that He needed to be about His Father's business. He went to Jerusalem with Joseph and Mary to the feast of the Passover. They assumed He was with relatives, but after searching for Jesus for three days, they found Him. But Jesus knew it was time for Him to be about His Father's business. Joseph and Mary knew Jesus was the Messiah, but God did not reveal to them when Jesus would begin His earthly ministry. Neither will God tell anyone what God has called you to do before He tells you. Other people can confirm, but He will always tell you first.

> And it came to pass, that after three days they found him in the temple, sitting in the midst of the doctors, both hearing them, and asking them questions. And all that heard him were astonished at his understanding and answers. And when they saw him, they were amazed: and his mother said unto him, Son, why hast thou thus dealt with us? Behold, thy father and I have sought thee sorrowing. And he said unto them, "How is it that ye sought me? Wist ye not that I must be about my Father's business? (Luke 2:46–49)

We can say that was the "call." But there was a time of preparation. Jesus went home and was subject to His mother and father. Eighteen years later, Jesus was baptized by John the Baptist. Afterward, the Spirit led Jesus into the wilderness to be tempted of the devil. Jesus resisted Satan's offers by speaking the Word of God. Jesus began His public ministry by selecting twelve men to take the message of repentance and the kingdom of God to the children of Abraham, Isaac, and Jacob.

Jesus discipled both men and women, who disseminated the "Good News" that Jesus was the Messiah and that the kingdom of God was at hand. Those who heard and believed their message also shared it until the whole known world was evangelized.

Naturally, Jesus's disciples were curious about the signs of His coming and the end of the world. He provided very specific details about the events that would take place. The early church diligently followed Jesus's commandment to preach the gospel of the kingdom.

You and I are the product of their faithfulness to preach it in all the world as a witness to all nations. Jesus is relying on the end-time church to continue running the race, lifting the torch high and lighting the path for others to come to the saving knowledge of Jesus Christ.

Jesus told the disciples, "And this gospel of the kingdom shall be preached in all the world for a witness unto all nations; and then shall the end come" (Matthew 24:14).

On the day of Pentecost, when the Holy Ghost was sent from God to empower the followers of Jesus Christ, female disciples were among the 120 in the upper room. These followers of Christ received the baptism of the Holy Ghost, along with the male disciples of Christ.

"These all continued with one accord in prayer and supplication, with the women, and Mary the mother of Jesus and with his brethren" (Acts 1:14). "And they were all filled with the Holy Ghost, and began to speak with other tongues, as the Spirit gave them utterance" (Acts 2:4). There are other scriptures that specifically name women as apostles. Priscilla and her husband, Aquila, established a church in their home. "The churches of Asia salute you. Aquila and Priscilla salute you much in the Lord, with the church that is in their house" (1 Corinthians 16:19). This husband-and-wife team were church planters. They were also apostles, who ministered and traveled with the apostle Paul. Andronicus and Junia were not named among the twelve disciples, and neither was Paul; however, the apostle Paul recognized their apostolic calling.

"Salute Andronicus and Junia, my kinsmen, and fellow prisoners, who are of note among the apostles, who also were in Christ before me" (Romans 16:7).

Junia was a female apostle who became a follower of Jesus Christ before Paul. Priscilla and Junia were women "sent by God," along with Paul, Aquila, and Andronicus. Jesus told us to pray that the Lord of the harvest send forth laborers into His harvest. Jesus did not say to send men but laborers. The King James dictionary definition of the word labor is "toil, To labor; to work; to exert strength with pain and fatigue of body or mind, particularly of the body, with efforts of some continuance or duration."[4]

"Then saith he unto his disciples, The harvest truly is plenteous, but the labourers are few; Pray ye therefore the Lord of the harvest, that he will send forth labourers into his harvest" (Matthew 9:37, 38).

Church, it is harvesttime! Souls are perishing every second. Millions of people are going into the abyss of hell, while the church is arguing and debating about the gender issues involving the ministry gifts in the Body of Christ. The gifts were sent by God, and He sent them to perfect the saints. The gifts in the Body of Christ are for the work of the ministry, to strengthen and encourage the body of Christ. Jesus's perfect will for His body of baptized believers is that we all come into the unity of the faith. This can only be accomplished by truly loving one another, dying to ourselves, and submitting our all to Christ.

The devil has done a prodigious job of deceiving the Body of Christ in believing the detrimental lie that scripture validates that it is unbiblical for women to serve as prelates, having oversight leadership roles in the church.

Jesus knew He would soon leave the earth. His time with His disciples was coming to an end. His heart was extremely heavy. He knelt down and prayed for all who would believe in Him through their words.

"And now I am no more in the world, but these are in the world, and I come to thee. Holy Father, keep through thine own name those whom thou hast given me, that they may be one, as we are one" (John 17:11).

Was He only praying for male disciples? Would He exclude women who had sat at His feet, supported His ministry, carried their children, and followed Him to hear His teachings? Isn't the same charge in Mark 16:15, to go, given to every follower of Jesus Christ?

"And these signs shall follow them that believe; In my name shall they cast out devils; they shall speak with new tongues; They shall take up serpents; and if they drink any deadly thing, it shall not hurt them; they shall lay hands on the sick, and they shall recover."

With over 7.5 billion people in the world, there is plenty of work to be done. Even if every male ´´disciple went into all the world to proclaim the gospel, they could never reach everyone. There is a tremendous need for more laborers to go. Every believer is to become a "fisher of men."

ENDURANCE CONDITIONING

I WAS YOUNG, A WIFE AND mother of three children, two teens and one preteen. I was active in the church as a junior high Sunday school teacher and a deaconess and sang in the choir when the Lord anointed me with the ministry gift of an evangelist. I told Ted, "Honey, the Lord is calling me into another area of ministry, and I feel compelled to fulfill it."

He said, "What do you feel God is calling you to do?"

I said, "He's calling me to win souls, to compel people to accept Jesus." I hadn't thought about how he would react to my announcement, but I certainly wasn't ready for his response.

He said, "Jan, if you start preaching, I'm going to leave you!" I was stunned and quite surprised to hear him threaten to leave me if I preached the gospel. I became very quiet and waited for the counsel of the Holy Spirit. When I opened my mouth to respond, the words flowed from my lips in such a gentle way, I knew it was the Holy Spirit speaking through me. I said, "Ted, I love you very much, but I must obey God. If you leave me because I preach the gospel of Jesus Christ, then you will just have to leave me."

God settled the matter, and he finally said, "Jan, do what you have to do." He became my strongest supporter and encouraged me in my ministry. He was my confidant, and I would often ask him to pray for me when I went into the streets to minister to the homeless or at one of the district churches. In 1974, I went before the jurisdictional state licensing board of the church denomination we were in, and I received my license as an evangelist missionary.

It wasn't long afterward that Ted received the baptism of the Holy Ghost and totally committed his life to the service of the Lord, and we began our journey together as ministers of the Lord Jesus Christ. Youth ministry was our passion. We transported vanloads of children to church every Sunday. Our children's friends became our converts, and eventually, their parents started going to church and entire households were saved.

A couple of years later, God called us as rural missionaries. We were traveling back and forth across the country, assisting pastors with their churches. The Lord sent us to newly planted churches or struggling established churches. Angela, our daughter, worked with the children's ministry, and our two sons, Cliff and Terrance, played saxophones. Ted was a gifted jack-of-all-trades, with many skills. He was indeed a pastor's deacon, meaning he was a man filled with the Holy Ghost and served wholeheartedly. I taught Sunday school, preached, organized special services, and continued to reach souls in the community.

Our first assignment was working with a newly formed church in a small rural town. The pastor was young and inexperienced. Except for a couple of other families, most of the people attending the church were the pastor's family. We knew we were on an assignment from the Lord, and we always prayed for God to lead us and go before us. I learned very early in ministry that just because people say they are followers of Jesus and teach from the same Bible does not necessarily mean they are born again or obedient followers of Christ. I began to understand what Jesus meant in Matthew 7:20 when He said, "Wherefore by their fruit ye shall know them."

I quickly discovered how necessary the Holy Spirit was in the work of the ministry when going into certain regions and dealing with situations that are unfamiliar. I never encountered the kind of demonic activity that was taking place in that rural community. I didn't know anything about witchcraft, but I learned it was a common practice in the South, used to control people and influence situations. I also discovered there were various kinds of territorial spirits that controlled different regions throughout the world.

Surprisingly, the practice of witchcraft was so common that it was not unusual for members of the church to continue to dabble in it, even after accepting Christ. I received a telephone call from a young girl from the church, telling me someone put a curse on one of the girls who attended the church and she was taken to a woman in the area who practiced witchcraft for the purpose of removing it. When I heard that, I realized they were not aware witchcraft was not of God, and I referred them back to the pastor and warned them to avoid anything to do with the occult. I read Deuteronomy 18 to them and prayed for God to keep them from evil.

> There shall not be found among you any one that maketh his son or his daughter to pass through the fire, or that useth divination, or an observer of times or an enchanter or a witch, Or a charmer, or a consulter with familiar spirits, or a wizard, or a necromancer. For all that do these things are an abomination unto the Lord; and because of these abominations, the Lord thy God doeth drive them out from before thee. Thou shalt be perfect with the Lord thy God. For these nations, which thou shalt possess, harkened unto observers of times, and unto diviners; but as for thee the Lord thy God hath not suffered thee so to do. (Deuteronomy 18:10–14)

Later that evening, I received a call from the pastor. He was extremely angry with me. He banned me from his church and said he would tell all the other pastors in the area to keep me out of their churches. I was shocked and heartbroken. I told Ted what had happened, and we prayed for God to forgive the pastor and to heal my troubled mind and broken heart. While I was praying, the Lord revealed to me that the devil had been exposed and was coming after me because I shared God's Word denouncing the occult. I told Ted and the children it did not matter that I was not welcome in his church, and even if I was blackballed from all the churches, I would still be faithful to God's Word and always teach and preach the truth.

The Lord was teaching me that He is faithful and will fight my battles for me. He taught me that He never expects us to fight our own battles. We prayed, and the Lord led us to contact a pastor in town. We explained to him what had happened, and he said, "Oh, I've known that fellow all my life. Don't worry about him. You and your family are welcome at our church."

Everyone warmly received us, and we rolled our sleeves up and went to work. We were sent to this precious pastor to be a blessing and to be blessed. We faithfully worked with the pastor for two years. When our assignment was over at a particular church, God would send us on another assignment, to another rural town, to another church.

From my travels as a rural missionary, I became aware there are many practices handed down from ancestors to their children that are an abomination to God. People are perishing because of not knowing God's Word. Unless pastors and teachers teach the people from the Old Testament, even well-meaning, churchgoing, professing Christians will ignorantly engage in ungodly practices, believing it is the work of the Holy Spirit. Satan is very good at the art of deception, deceiving millions of unsuspecting souls who have little or no knowledge of scriptures regarding the strategies of the devil and how to overcome them. The fear and reverence of the one true and living God is missing in our homes, churches, and communities; therefore, people are perishing, and the Body of Christ has been called to save them from destruction.

"The fear of the Lord is the beginning of wisdom: a good understanding have all they that do his commandments: his praise endureth for ever" (Psalm 111:10).

We moved to a small rural area about thirty-five miles from Little Rock, Arkansas. Most of the people living in the town were poor, and the majority were black. There was a small general store operated by a white man.

One day, I walked into the store, and the Holy Spirit said, "Tell him that I've been blessing him, but unless he stops oppressing the people, I will withdraw my blessings."

There were quite a few customers in the store, so I left the store, with the intention of returning later. A few days went by, and my head started spinning. I couldn't get any relief. I felt like I was on the fastest merry-go round in the world. I rolled from side to side on the bed, praying for the Lord to heal me. Then I heard the Lord say, "When you do what I told you to do, I will deliver you."

I said, "Father, what did You tell me to do?"

He said, "I told you to tell the owner of the store, if he did not stop oppressing the poor, I would withdraw my blessings."

I staggered off the bed, slipped my shoes on, and informed Ted I had to take a message to the store owner from God. I ran down the road as fast as I could, staggering because of the dizziness.

When I arrived at the store, I took a deep breath and entered. Immediately, the spinning stopped. I was relieved when I saw no one else was in the store. I stepped to the counter and glanced down. On the counter next to the cash register was a Bible. I looked up, and our eyes met. I said, "Thus said the Lord, I have been blessing you, but unless you stop oppressing the people, I will withdraw my blessings from you."

He stared back at me and said, "Okay."

I turned and walked out of the store. That experience taught me about the grace of God and the love He has for His people. I don't know the details of what happened to the store owner, but we visited the town two years later, and the store was closed.

A couple of months after I gave the message to the store owner, the Lord said, "Tell your husband it is time to move out of this town." I said, "Lord, that means we have to rent a truck, load up everything, and move again. I am so tired of moving."

I never said anything to Ted about my conversation with the Lord. Early Easter morning, while it was still dark, a loud chime sounded in my ear, waking me up. I smelled smoke, but I thought the scent was coming from the wood stove in the den.

All of a sudden, I heard the Holy Spirit say, "Get up, get the broom, go to the bathroom, and push the attic door open." When I pushed the door open, I saw the entire attic was engulfed in flames. I shouted loudly to wake Ted and ran to the children's bedroom to lead them out of the house. Miraculously, we were all blessed to get out safely. Ted grabbed the water hose and started trying to control the flames. The volunteer firemen and neighbors helped us put the fire out. We were truly blessed because the flames had been confined to the attic. We cleaned up the water damage and aired the house out. Ted suggested that I take the children to church because it was Easter and he would stay home and watch the house. We were told that flames sometimes hide and it was important to keep an eye out for any smoke coming from the attic.

The children and I had been in church for an hour when one of the neighbors rushed through the door and told me our house was engulfed in flames. As I went, I prayed, "Lord, please keep Ted safe." I was so relieved when I saw he was okay, but my heart sank when I saw the house had burned down to the ground. Then I remembered what God said to me: "Tell your husband it is time to move from this town." Then I heard the Lord say, "Move, Janice. You don't need a truck."

Amazingly, our photo album survived the flames. The pictures were slightly scorched. Except for our car, all other possessions were gone. The angels of the Lord woke me up with the sound of a chime and saved our lives. God protected us and delivered our family from the shadow of death. While I stood there looking at the smoldering ashes, I repented and felt remorse because this could have been avoided if I would have obeyed the Lord. From that experience, I learned there are serious consequences for rebelling against God and exercising your own will over God's.

After the fire, I told Ted about my conversation with God. He said, "Jan, you should have told me. I would have moved." He knew me very well and over the years had witnessed God using me prophetically. Shortly after we were married, he realized he had married a woman whom God frequently talked with, through the Holy Spirit, the scriptures, dreams, and visions. I didn't know it at the time, but I was in the School of the Holy Ghost, and I had just failed my first test. Failing the test was dangerous not only for me but for my family and those God would use me to minister to. I developed a reverent fear of the Almighty God of all creation. I knew I must listen and obey even when I didn't understand or didn't want to do what He told me to do. God had placed a prophetic mantle upon my life, and I did not know how to effectively operate in it. I hadn't heard anyone discuss the kind of experiences I was having with the Lord. The Holy Spirit was teaching me to recognize, listen, and submit to the will of God.

Even in my disobedience, God continued to show His mercy toward us. Our neighbors opened their home to us, offering us a place to stay until the insurance claim was settled. Everyone was so supportive and charitable. Southerners are very compassionate and generous people. People from the surrounding counties heard about the fire and donated clothes, food, and furniture.

HOPE

ALTHOUGH TED AND I DID not want to raise our children in the city, we felt God leading us to look for a home there. We found an old two-story Victorian-style home with what I call "character," and we bought it. Our neighbor was a young white woman with two young children. I'd speak to her when going in and out of the house but never formally introduced myself. One day, all that changed.

I returned home from shopping when the Holy Spirit spoke to me with such force, "Go next door to your neighbor's house!" I quickly put the bags on the counter, hurried next door, and knocked on the door. A tearful young woman peeped through the cracked door. I introduced myself and asked if she was all right. She shook her head to indicate she wasn't. I said, "The Holy Spirit sent me to check on you. May I come in?" She hesitated, but I kept talking, and eventually, she opened the door. I sat down across from her. I could see the pain in her eyes. She had dark circles under her eyes from lack of sleep, and her eyes were red and swollen from crying. Massive tears flowed down her face as she told me about being abandoned by her husband and rejected by her family because she had married a black man. She was depressed and in despair. She said, "I am broke and don't have money to feed my kids or pay my rent. My car is not running, and I don't know what to do. My kids and I would be better off dead. Before you knocked on the door, I had decided to take the life of my children and kill myself."

I rose from where I was sitting, sat next to her, and held her in my arms until God's love flowed into her heart as she bitterly wept. I told her how much Jesus loved her and that He would turn her life around if she would only believe God to provide for her and her children.

Later, she told me she was brought up in a Christian home and had accepted Jesus as her Savior but had strayed away from God. I encouraged her to rededicate her life to Jesus. She knelt with me and cried, "Jesus, forgive me of my sins and restore my soul." That night, God saved the lives of two innocent children and a precious young mother. I assured her of God's love and my love for her. Her relationship with her heavenly Father was restored. She and the children went to church with us, and she was baptized with the Holy Ghost. My family became her family. The Lord was faithful to provide for all her needs. He turned her mourning into dancing and gave her a garment of praise for the spirit of heaviness.

Her husband returned home, and the family continued to grow in the Lord. The Lord led us to buy that particular house. He later revealed to me that the preservation of this family was the reason He told me to move out of the town we were living in.

God wanted to use me to speak life over the young woman's circumstances, giving her hope through Christ. A year later, we were released from our rural ministry to return to the West Coast. We went back to our home church and continued to work in the ministry with my uncle.

THE COMMISSION

IN 1993, I WORKED AS an administrator for a drug and alcohol program. One afternoon, I left my office to go to lunch. While driving, I had an encounter with the Lord. He said, "Janice, why is it you are not obeying Me?" When my heavenly Father asks me that question, I've learned from experience that I'd forgotten what He said.

I said, "What am I not doing that You told me to do?"

You see, I thought I was in the will of God. I ministered at church, conducted revivals, and was a conference speaker, and the clients in the drug and alcohol treatment program I managed were recovering, families were being restored, and many clients had accepted Christ as their Savior.

Once I heard a young evangelist say, "There are a lot of good things you may be doing, but they are not necessarily the things God told you to do." That was where I was.

God said, "I have called you to be a spiritual leader. I am calling you to establish a church and to pastor My people."

I said, "But, God, they won't receive me. I am a woman."

He said, "Who gave you life?"

I said, "You did."

He said, "Who can take your life?"

I said, "You can, Father."

He said, "Why should I let you live, if you don't obey Me?" I suddenly realized once again, I had allowed the traditions of men to impede my moving forward with what God had called me to do. At that point, I realized God had given me life for one purpose: to do His will. The Lord also revealed to me how critical it was for me to step into my pastoral calling. He showed me a vision of young people bound by demonic spirits, weeping and crying for deliverance. Then the Lord said something that brought great fear upon me. He said, "Unless you do what I have called you to do, your children will go into captivity." That being said, the Lord had my undivided attention.

I drove back to my office and wrote out my resignation letter. When I arrived home, I was hesitant to tell Ted what God had said for fear of what he would say. But I had a reverent fear of God and had to trust Him to deal with Ted. I shared with him what God had said, and to my amazement, God had been speaking to him about establishing a church. He said, "Jan, there is a little church building on the other side of the railroad tracks."

I said, "Ted, why didn't you tell me about the church before?" He said, "I've been telling you for three months, but you weren't listening." We drove to the church. It was an old adobe church building. Later, I found out the building was a historical site. Now it was nothing but a shell. Graffiti was all over the outside of the building, windows were broken out, and the entrance was boarded up. But when I stepped out of the car and my foot hit the concrete, the Lord spoke to me and said, "Janice, turn this place into a house of prayer for all people."

We were blessed to locate the owner of the building. I said, "The Lord wants a house of prayer in this community because He loves the people. How much are you asking to rent this building?"

He said, "I can't fix it up, but if you want it, I will rent it to you for two hundred dollars a month."

Ted and I didn't think we would have any problems getting help to renovate the building; after all, Ted was a jack-of-all-trades. He physically could not do all the hard work, but he could supervise and teach others to do it. I also had a daily radio program on a local Christian station, and I thought the Lord would touch the hearts of some of the listeners to help us renovate the building. I put out a Macedonia call for manpower. Boy, was I ever wrong. I requested help over the radio and went to various community organizations and other churches, trying to solicit help, but no one responded.

I went to the city to get the permit to occupy the building. They thought I had lost my mind and offered to give me another building. They said, "Why do you want to establish a church in that area? There's nothing but drugs and gangs in that neighborhood."

I said, "That's the place Jesus wants to establish the church. He loves the people."

I knew God wanted to perform a miracle in that community. I went on a fast for three weeks, put a blanket down on the concrete floor of the sanctuary, and prayed. I prayed for divine help because without it, there was no way that old dilapidated building could be repaired. Ted and I did not have money for the repairs. We were walking by faith, trusting the Lord to provide everything. It was His work, and we were being obedient. During the time I was fasting and praying, I could literally visualize the souls of men, women, and little boys and girls. My fasting and praying resulted in the Holy Spirit instructing Ted to start working on the building. People in the neighborhood started coming by, asking questions, wondering what a short, little black woman was doing in their neighborhood. The amazing thing was this building was in the barrio, where the oldest Mexican families settled and raised their families. Neither Ted nor I spoke Spanish.

We serve a God who does extraordinary things, in unexpected ways, in order that we may know there is no God like Him and nothing is impossible for Him. I learned over the years to trust God to provide all the plans, resources, and wisdom needed for the work. There was a great deal of work to be done in the sanctuary, and I was eager to get started. We fixed up a small area near the bathroom for prayer and Bible study. We handed out flyers around town and posted the announcement about the Bible study on the front of the church. I was excited and prayerfully waited to see who would come. As the hour drew near, I saw a man and his son walking toward the church. This man and his son became our second and third members Each week, more members of his family came. He pitched in and helped with the work. The Lord sent two precious men who were professional plasterers and painting contractors. These highly skilled, gifted men joined the church, and God miraculously brought light to a community that was overshadowed with darkness. I remember the first Sunday, we had service in the sanctuary. I stood behind the podium, looking out at the people sitting before me, and I wept. They were tears of joy. These precious people were the souls God had shown me while I fasted and prayed.

The first thing the Lord instructed me to do was to dedicate a room for prayer, a solitary, consecrated place where people could spend time with the Lord. He told me He would hear and answer the prayers of those who called upon Him in that room. When I shared the news about the prayer room with my oldest sister, she said, "Jan, God told me to pay for everything. Let me know how much you need."

My sister is a woman of prayer, and God had given her the assignment to finance the prayer room. It was absolutely beautiful, and when anyone stepped through the door, the comfort of the Holy Spirit was present. There were many testimonies of answered prayers from those who called upon God in the prayer room. We witnessed God doing many miracles in the lives of those who attended the church. People from as far away as sixty miles heard that we had a prayer room and about the miracles that God was performing in the lives of the people. During the week, people from other churches and cities came, for the purpose of praying in the prayer room.

I believe in the power of prayer, and when it comes to working for the Lord, it is essential to receive all instructions from Him; otherwise, our labor will be in vain and very difficult. The church belongs to Christ, and we are stewards. Jesus establishes churches to bless the city or town where they are planted. We not only interceded for the people in the community but always prayed for God's blessings upon the city officials, church leadership, schools, businesses, and families living in the city. It wasn't long before most of the gang members and drug dealers in the area disappeared. Peace and safety were restored to the community. When Jesus moves into an area, darkness must flee.

I was led to start an after-school program to provide a safe place for children ages six to sixteen. Miraculously, God provided the resources and everything we needed to run the program. We organized sports, board games, and field trips and offered tutoring and cooking, sewing, computer, and automobile maintenance classes. But most important, we introduced the children to their Savior, Jesus Christ. All of the children who regularly attended the program gained an understanding of the purpose for Jesus's death and His glorious resurrection. After hearing the simple gospel of Christ, every child received Jesus as his or her Savior. Parents saw the positive changes in their children, and their souls were stirred when they heard their children singing songs about Jesus and discussing what they learned from listening to Bible stories.

We were also blessed to minister to women from the Vietnamese community. A minister of our church invited several young women to our outreach activities. They had many questions, and when we shared the gospel of Jesus Christ with them, they gave their lives to Him. The transforming presence of the living God brought peace where there was despair, favor where there was disdain, and prosperity where there was poverty.

Our congregation rapidly grew to over a hundred people in a period of six months. At every altar appeal, people came forward to accept Christ. The sick were healed, and people prospered financially. Children were growing in their knowledge of God and excelling in school. The multicultural congregation's love for Jesus and one another was evident by a spirit of unity within the church. It was an amazing glimpse of heaven on the earth. The Lord truly blessed the work.

The Holy Spirit led me to establish a school of ministry to train and equip members of the congregation to help with the growing ministry and to go out to reach more souls for Jesus. Some children in the area were performing below grade level, and some were being suspended from public school because of disciplinary problems. Other children were school ready but too young to attend public school. The Holy Spirit placed this burden on my heart, and I established a pre-K–12 day school. The children excelled in their studies and became quite disciplined.

From my years of experience working as a substance abuse counselor, I knew the urgency of getting people with an addiction history into a biblically based recovery group immediately after they received Christ. The group provided them with biblical spiritual tools and wisdom on how to recognize, take authority over, and break the relapse cycle. Addictions of any kind have a demonic root cause. The Holy Spirit reveals the root and the anointing of God destroys it, setting the captive free.

THE TEST

MERCIFUL GOD, COMPASSIONATE HEALER

FOUR YEARS AFTER TED AND I planted the church, we went through what I call a "Job" experience, a period of temptation, sifting, loss, pain, and mental torment. Hopelessness shadowed every waking hour for months.

It all began one day while I was tutoring a single mother and her son, when suddenly I felt a heavy thump in my left breast. It felt like a bowling ball had been thrust into my chest. After a few seconds, the pain subsided, and I quickly ended the session and drove a couple of blocks to my house. By the time I arrived, the pain was completely gone, but I was weak. I thought if I could get some sleep, I would probably feel better in the morning. When I woke up the next morning, I felt exhausted so I stayed in bed. I drifted off into a light sleep and felt my spirit leave my body. I didn't feel any pain, but I was extremely tired. My spirit stood by the side of the bed and looked at my body lying there. Ted was walking into the bathroom when he suddenly stopped, turned, and looked at me. He rushed to the side of the bed and called my name. My spirit stood by watching. He called louder and began shaking me. At that point, my spirit returned to my body. I took a deep breath, and my eyes opened up. Ted wrapped me in a blanket and took me to the hospital. To my surprise, the doctor said I had suffered a mild heart attack. I spent a couple of days in the hospital while they monitored my heart and performed diagnostic tests. The saints of God were praying for me. God heard their prayers because I received my healing.

I had never experienced such helplessness. The adversary was attacking my mind. I suffered depression, and a constant stream of tears flowed from the corners of my eyes. I knew I was in crisis and needed someone to speak to me about spiritual things. I needed to hear the life-giving Word. I asked the nurse to arrange for the hospital chaplain to visit me. A few hours later, a soft-spoken man entered my room, pulled a chair close to the bed, and introduced himself as a chaplain. He said, "I understand you asked to see me."

I said, "Yes, thank you so much for coming. I am a pastor. I am lying in bed feeling like I have disappointed God."

He said, "Why do you say that?"

I said, "A precious member of our congregation is in another hospital battling cancer, and I promised her I would be there for her because she has no family."

He said, "What is your prayer life like?"

I said, "I pray every morning at three o'clock."

He said, "Who do you pray for?"

I shared my prayer list, and when I finished, he said, "Hmm, you forgot someone, didn't you?"

I said, "Who?"

He said, "Yourself?"

When I heard those words, it was as though the retainer wall of a dike burst, causing an impetuous torrent. Previous to the chaplain's visit, a constant flow of tears trickled down my face, but after being reminded God was concerned about me, I felt a deluge of tears flow down my face. Once I composed myself, he said, "Show me your hands." I held my hands out. He said, "I don't see any nail prints in your hands. God never intended for you to become a sacrificial lamb. He called you to teach and preach the gospel, leading people to Christ by example."

I thought about what the chaplain said and analyzed what I had been doing that wore me down. I soon realized I was patterning myself after my uncle who was a pastor and superintendent.

Most of my life, I had observed my uncle's pastoral style. He was a "father pastor," who allowed the people and district leaders to depend on him to meet their basic needs because he loved people and was compassionate and generous. I had developed that same style of trying to "rescue" not only the members of the congregation but people in the community. That experience taught me about the amazing grace of God. I will forever be deeply grateful and appreciative for godly men and women who serve as chaplains. They are truly blessings not only to the followers of Jesus Christ but to all people.

It took several weeks before I regained my strength. Still unable to attend services or return to school, I spent my days reading my Bible but found it difficult to concentrate. I listened to praise and worship music and watched a little Christian television.

For years, I had financially supported Christian television but only understood the incredible blessing God gave to the world by sending the message of hope through the airwaves. Christian television is a powerful outreach tool God is using to enable the Body of Christ to go into all the world and preach the gospel. Thank God for the choice servants He called to the media ministry.

The devil was taking full advantage of my infirmity by filling my mind with guilt and feelings of uselessness. He was doing a great job of oppressing me to the point I prayed for God to take me to heaven. I didn't want to stay in this world if there was nothing I could do for the kingdom of God. Early Sunday morning, I turned on the television, and Bishop T. D. Jakes was ministering. He pointed his finger at the camera and said, "There is a pastor watching me right now, and you have been asking God to take you home, but I was sent here to tell you to stop asking, because your work is not over; you are not going anywhere."

I dropped to my knees and cried, "Lord, forgive me for my lack of trust. Let Your will be done. Yes, Lord, whatever You want to do with my life. Have Your way."

The following Sunday, I walked into the church and experienced extreme joy to once again be back in the assembly. Too many times, Christians fail to appreciate how precious their brothers and sisters in the Lord are until it's too late. I know it was the love and prayers of the Body of Christ that moved the heart of God, resulting in my recovery.

I asked the Lord, "Why did I go through that experience?" and He said, "Grace."

I said, "Grace, unmerited favor?"

He said, "Janice, man has nothing to do with My kingdom. I am sovereign. I call who I want to call, use who I want to use, and send who I want to send and heal who I want to heal." After the Lord raised me up, He released a "grace anointing" upon my life and ministry. I soon realized it was good for me to go through that experience. The sickness, depression, and state of total dependency on God had increased my reverence for God and my intimacy with Him and my precious Jesus. Suffering serves as a catalyst for divine service to the Lord. Dying to self is the spiritual goal. Apostle Paul spoke about Christ suffering and the fruit it produces. "Though he were a Son, yet learned he obedience by the things which he suffered" (Hebrews 5:8). After my suffering experience, I echoed the psalmist's words when he wrote, "It is good for me that I have been afflicted; that I might learn thy statutes" (Psalm 119:71).

I also learned another invaluable lesson from the scriptures during my illness. It was about the "Sabbath rest." I grew up in a denominational church and just assumed when we went to church on Sunday, that was the Sabbath rest. The Holy Spirit said, "Many of God's people are dying prematurely and are afflicted because of violating the Sabbath."

I cried, "Holy Spirit, teach me about the Sabbath. I don't understand the mind of God regarding the Sabbath."

He answered, and I entered the School of the Holy Ghost. This a name given to me by the Holy Spirit when He is teaching spiritual truths, revealing mysteries, and giving revelation to believers. Jesus did not leave us alone when He went to heaven. He sent the comforter, teacher, and guide, the Holy Spirit, to help us. There is so much more we need to know about the kingdom work on earth. Jesus said, before He went to heaven,

> I have yet many things to say unto you, but ye cannot bear them now. Howbeit when he, the Spirit of truth, is come, he will guide you into all truth: for he shall not speak of himself; but whatsoever he shall hear, that shall he speak: and he will shew you things to come. He shall glorify me: for he shall receive of mine, and shall shew it unto you. (John 16:12–14)

The Holy Spirit took me through the Bible from Genesis to Revelation. He opened my understanding, regarding the blessing of the Sabbath for all creation and the reason God commanded to keep it holy.

The Spirit of truth revealed a loving Father's thoughts for the good of all creation. God's will for humankind was for them to possess sustained optimal relational, physical, and mental health; superior mental clarity; and a close and intimate relationship with Him.

I discovered Satan had deceived me for years and was literally wearing me out with perpetual work—eighteen-hour days, seven days a week, 365 days a year. I am convinced a lying spirit entered the world, altering the Sabbath rest from God's original purpose. The Sabbath rest is a perpetual covenant with the Only True and Living

God, YAHWAH, creator of everything seen and unseen. According to the KJV dictionary, *perpetual* has the following definition:

> PERPET'UAL, a. L. perpetuus, from perpes, perpetis; per and pes, from a root signifying to pass.
>
> 1. Never ceasing; continuing forever in future time; destined to be eternal; as a perpetual covenant; a perpetual statute. Literally true with respect to the decrees of the Supreme Being.
> 2. Continuing or continued without intermission; uninterrupted; as a perpetual stream; the perpetual action of the heart and arteries.
> 3. Permanent; fixed; not temporary; as a perpetual law or edict; perpetual love or amity, perpetual incense. Ex.30.
> 4. Everlasting; endless.[5]

Prior to my illness, I felt good, with no known health issues. But unknowingly, I was in danger of dying prematurely or suffering some debilitating disease because of lack of knowledge and understanding of God's Word regarding the Sabbath.

Because I am a Christian, I was raised to attend church on Sunday. I was taught that Sunday was the Sabbath, the holy day. It was a day for worshipping and fellowshipping with family and brothers and sisters in Christ. All preparation for Sunday was done on Saturday. It was during my illness that the Holy Spirit taught me the truth. Remember, I cried out to God. I had heard so many conflicting messages and did not know who was right, although I was a pastor and had been in ministry for many years. I later discovered I was keeping the traditions of men, rather than following the teachings of scriptures.

> Thus the heavens and the earth was finished, and all the host of them. And on the seventh day God ended his work which he had made; and he rested on the seventh day from all his work which he had made. And God blessed the seventh day, and sanctified it: because that in

> it he had rested from all his work which God created and made. (Genesis 2:1–3)

God authored the Ten Commandments and wrote them with His own hand on a stone tablet for the welfare of all His creation. The Ten Commandments are perpetual and do not change. God said,

> Remember the sabbath day to keep it holy. Six days shalt thou labour and do all thy work: But the seventh day is the sabbath of the Lord thy God: in it thou shalt not do any work, thou, nor thy son, nor thy daughter, thy manservant, nor thy maidservant, nor thy cattle, nor thy stranger that is within thy gates: For in six days the Lord made heaven and earth, the sea, and all that in them is, and rested the seventh day: wherefore the Lord blessed the sabbath day, and hallowed it. (Exodus 10:8–11)

I discovered the seventh day is Saturday, not Sunday. I set out to discover the truth. I wanted the answer to the question, "If Sunday is not the Lord's Sabbath, who changed it from Saturday to Sunday?" My research revealed that The International Organization for Standardization (IOS) 1988, changed Sunday to the seventh day of the week and Saturday to the sixth day of the week in order that Monday would be the first day of the week. According to the Bible and the Hebrew calendar, Sunday is the first day of the week. Jesus's body lay in the sepulcher from Friday evening, the Sabbath, to Sunday, the first day of the week. According to Genesis, sunrise does not mark the beginning of a new day. Rather sundown is the beginning of a new day.

"And God called the light Day, and the darkness he called Night. And the evening and the morning were the first day" (Genesis 1:5).

"The first day of the week cometh Mary Magdalene early, when it was yet dark, unto the sepulcher, and seeth the stone taken away from the sepulcher" (John 20:1).

Jesus was resurrected on Sunday, the first day of the week, revealing that the Sabbath, the seventh day of the week, is a holy day unlike any other day of the week.

The IOS, which was formed in 1947, changed Sunday from the first day of the week to the seventh day of the week. After discovering how man has changed times and seasons established by God, I took a bold step to obey God rather than the traditions I had been taught and began to observe the Sabbath, to rest on the seventh day from work and entertainment, which resulted in a more intimate relationship with my heavenly Father; spiritual growth; peace in my soul, heart, and mind; increased productivity during the week; and more mental clarity and focus. I have more energy, fewer illnesses, and the ability to recover quickly from infirmities that attack my body.

> The definition of rest, according to the KJV dictionary, is cessation of motion or action of any kind, and applicable to any body or being; as rest from labor; rest from mental exertion; rest of body and mind. A body is at rest, when it ceases to move; the mind is at rest, when it ceases to be disturbed or agitated: the sea is never at rest. 2 Quiet; repose; a state free from motion or disturbance; a state of reconciliation to God.[6]

I consider this an important topic for this book because the Holy Spirit taught me about the "Sabbath rest."

God not only created man in His image and in His likeness, but He had holy men who were scribes to record His instructions to humankind on how man could live a long, healthy, peaceful, productive, and prosperous life on the earth. I often compare the instructions in the Holy Bible to a manufacturer's user's manual for a car. However, most consumers don't read the manual until they have a problem. Sadly, many Christians do not seek the counsel of God from the Bible until there is a crisis. Despite every demonic effort to destroy the Holy Bible, mankind has not been successful because the Bible is the mind of God, it is the living Word, and it is hope being revealed to a hopeless world. The Bible is a collection of commandments, statutes, poetry, prophecies, wisdom, parables, epistles, history, and revelations. It is the Word becoming flesh, the bread of life, the living water; it is Jesus our Lord. The Bible teaches humanity how to experience heaven on earth and obtain eternal life. It provides simple, clear examples and instructions to humankind on how to walk under an open heaven and obtain favor from God and humankind in every area of life while on the earth. It further provides the promises that await us if we choose to follow His instructions. The Bible also tells us what happens when we reject God's counsel and establish our own righteousness. Should we ever say to the Creator, "We have a consensus; we don't quite believe it is economically feasible to rest on the seventh day (Sabbath) and then worship on Sunday (the first day of the week). We will lose millions of dollars if we observe the seventh day, keeping it holy, and worship on the first day of the week. We will just tell the whole world the Sabbath is Sunday instead of Saturday."

It takes real courage to follow the teachings of scripture, but Jesus said,

"And fear not them which kill the body, but are not able to kill the soul: but rather fear him which is able to destroy both soul and body in hell" (Matthew 10:28).

We must continually be reminded that there is a war going on. The battle is for the souls of humankind. Every leader in the Body of Christ is challenged with whether to obey God or man, but I encourage you to stand firm in the face of opposition and declare your commitment to Jesus like Apostle Peter, when he declared, "We ought to obey God rather than man" (Acts 5:29).

I was exhausted and was unknowingly shortening my life, abusing my body by denying it adequate rest. Although I spent most of my life going to church and listening to sermons, I never heard one message on the "principal commandment" the Creator gave to humankind for their benefit, the one basic commandment of God that brings forth optimum overall health of the spirit, soul, body, and mind. Jesus emphasized this little realized fact by stating who the Sabbath was made for and emphasizing His Lordship over the

Sabbath. "And he said unto them, The sabbath was made for man, and not man for the sabbath. Therefore the Son of man is Lord also over the sabbath" (Mark 2:27–28).

Please stay with me on this. This could save your life like it did mine. I had a grueling schedule. I was a wife, mother of three adult children, grandmother, and senior pastor of a church. I conducted and sometimes attended weekly prayer and Bible classes. I was the founder, administrator, and teacher of a small Christian K–12 school. I was a counselor and visited hospitals and jails and attended community and ministerial alliance meetings. I was literally working around the clock with a maximum of five or six hours of sleep at night. I ministered twice a month on Sunday and worked at the school Monday through Friday for eight hours. On Saturdays, I cleaned my house, did laundry, cooked, and occasionally went on an outing with the family and spent time praying, studying, fasting, and preparing for services on Sunday. Sunday evenings, I would spend time with my husband and work until late at night, preparing for my workweek. It was nonstop physical and mental stress. The sad thing is that I thought I was in the will of God. I soon found out I had been greatly deceived by the devil. His plans were to wear me out physically and to destroy my marriage, family, ministry, and to take my life. Praise God for revelation knowledge and discernment.

During the time I was bedridden from overworking, the Holy Spirit directed me to search out and study scriptures about the Lord's Sabbath for answers to questions I occasionally thought about concerning the Sabbath, such as "Why did God establish the Sabbath? How did God instruct humankind to keep the Sabbath? Did the finished work of Jesus Christ do away with the Sabbath? Is the Sabbath a commandment only for Israel? Will the Sabbath rest continue in the New Jerusalem?" As I began to study, I discovered the Lord's Sabbath was given to benefit humanity, not to punish us. I want to make it very clear that I am a Spirit-filled Christian who has kept the Lord's Sabbath rest since 1997. I fellowship with my brothers and sisters in Christ who worship on the Sabbath and Sunday. I just love my brothers and sisters in Christ. I do not have any schisms. But I have little tolerance for gross disrespect. God forbid if I allow Satan to cause me to withdraw from them because they choose to worship on the Sabbath or the first day of the week. Remember, the first followers of Jesus were Jewish.

"Now they which were scattered abroad upon the persecution that arose about Stephen travelled as far as Phenice, and Cyprus, and Antioch, preaching the word to none but unto the Jews only" (Acts 11:19, 20).

After Saul's (Paul) encounter with Jesus on the road to Damascus, the first place he went after the scales fell from his eyes and he was strengthened was to the synagogues. "And straightway he [Saul] preached in the synagogues, that he is the Son of God" (Acts 9:20).

The apostle Paul met with the followers of Jesus on the first day of the week (Sunday). "And upon the first day of the week, when the disciples came together to break bread, Paul preached unto them, ready to depart on the morrow; and continued his speech until midnight" (Acts 20:7).

They went to the temple on the Sabbath and met on the first day of the week. They continued to keep the Sabbath and the feast.

There are times when I spend the Sabbath quietly—resting, praying, and studying scriptures. When I attend services on the Sabbath, I fellowship for a while and return home to rest my mind and body. Before Jesus ascended to heaven, He clearly stated how to achieve salvation and how a person will receive damnation. "He that believeth and is baptized shall be saved, but he that believeth not shall be damned" (Mark 16:16).

Jesus said, "He that believeth on him is not condemned: but he that believeth not is condemned already, because he hath not believed in the name of the only begotten Son of God" (John 3:18).

Because of my obedience to the scriptures, my health was restored, I experienced sharper mental clarity and was more productive in six days of working than I was when I worked seven days a week. Although it is quite an adjustment socially to adapt to not being involved in recreational activities or doing housework and shopping on the seventh day, I have a deep sense of peace, knowing I am obeying God, and the evidence is that I am thriving in every area of my life. When I went to Israel in 2013 and 2016, I observed how the Sabbath was kept by the Israelis. Generally, it is a day of rest and going to the synagogue. After sundown on Saturday, the streets were filled with people bustling around, almost as though they were trying to make up for resting on the Sabbath.

From my observation of Sabbath keepers, they are much too busy and not really resting; consequently, many are sick and feeble. Sunday is the first day of the week, so they are busy, cleaning, washing, and working around the house or yard. They are lacking physical and mental rest. I am witnessing a great deal of sickness in the Body of Christ for those who worship on the Sabbath and on Sunday. I am of the opinion it is not only environmental but due to the violation of God's commandment to rest on the Sabbath day and to keep it holy.

The Lord's Sabbath is from Friday sundown, the seventh day of the week, to Saturday sundown. According to the creation account from the Bible, days did not start with the rising of the sun but when the sun went down in the evening. "And the evening and the morning were the first day" (Genesis 1:5).

Sunday is not the seventh day of the week, the Lord's Sabbath; it is the first day of the week, the day the Jewish New Testament Christians met and worshipped. Therefore, most Christian churches follow their example regarding gathering on Sunday to worship and fellowship, and Jesus rose on the first day of the week, a Sunday. "And upon the first day of the week, when the disciples came together to break bread, Paul preached unto them, ready to depart on the morrow; and continued his speech until midnight" (Acts 20:7).

It is important for both those who worship on the Sabbath and those who worship on Sunday to remember Jesus is with you. "For where two or three are gathered together in my name, there am I in the midst of them" (Matthew 18:20).

The Pharisees were always trying to trap Jesus, and they confronted Him about His disciples plucking ears of corn to eat as they walked through a cornfield. This is Jesus's response to their accusations.

> Have you not read so much as this, what David did, when himself was an hungered, and they which were with him; How he went into the house of God, and did take and eat the shewbread, and gave also to them that were with him; which it is not lawful to eat but for the priest alone? And he said unto them, That the Son of man is Lord also of the sabbath. (Luke 6:3–5)

When we consider the biblical definition of "rest," it is quite evident that the Sabbath rest is a gift from God that is beneficial to all life. God did not command that it be kept only by the Israelites. It was not to divide the Body of Christ but to make us one that the entire world would worship and serve the God of all creation, the God of the Sabbath rest. God spoke through the prophet Isaiah: "And it shall come to pass, that from one new moon to another, and from one sabbath to another, shall all flesh come to worship before me, saith the Lord" (Isaiah 66:23).

"Thy Kingdom come. Thy will be done on earth, as it is in Heaven" (Matthew 6:10).

GREAT DELIVERER

MY HUSBAND WAS CHALLENGED WITH severe chronic arthritis in his late thirties. Because of the severity of his condition, he was prescribed medication to manage the pain. He became dependent, and it resulted in a vicious cycle of deliverance and dependency that continued throughout most of his life.

This cycle began when he was involved in an accident with a bus in his early thirties. The next day, he went to work but left work early because of severe pains in his head. Unable to make it home, he stopped at the first doctor's office he saw. That encounter with the doctor dramatically altered the course of our lives. Ted told the doctor he had been sideswiped by a city bus on the way home from work. The doctor called an ambulance, and Ted was transported to the hospital. We didn't know until weeks later the doctor owned the hospital. I was quite concerned because Ted's behavior was unusual. I discovered later he was heavily medicated with psychotropics and narcotics. I didn't know what was happening, and every time I called the doctor's office or left a message, he wouldn't return my call.

One day, my husband called and said, "Jan, come get me out of here. The lady who came to clean my room asked me why I was in the hospital. When I told her, she said, 'Son, everyone who come into this hospital either end up in a mental institution or dead. If you are still in here when I come in tomorrow, I will throw you out the window myself.'"

I said, "Thank God for that woman. I'm going to pick up Arlene [his sister], and we will be there shortly."

I was eight months pregnant with my second child, and I knew I needed the support of his sister. I called her and told her that Ted was in trouble and we must get him out of that hospital. I contacted the hospital to tell them I was taking my husband to another hospital and was on my way and to have the discharge papers ready. By the time we arrived, Ted was heavily sedated. We asked for a wheelchair, and they refused to give us one. My sister-in-law and I had to literally drag him out of the hospital on our shoulders. We took him straight to the emergency room in the hospital where I was going to have the baby.

The doctor examined Ted and shared his findings with us. He seemed very uncomfortable, and tears were welling up in his eyes as he explained that Ted had a slight concussion, but x-rays ruled out any broken bones or internal injuries. He said, "Mrs. Turner, just like there are rotten eggs in other businesses, the doctor your husband was under was unethical and was unnecessarily giving him drugs that were very dangerous and addictive. I am so sorry you and your family are having to go through this. The only thing that I can find that is of great concern is that your husband was given psychotropics and narcotics for two weeks. I am going to watch him for a couple of hours, flush his system out, and send him home. But I have to warn you, he is going to go through a very difficult time because of the withdrawals, which may include hallucinations, and he may never be the same. From what you told me about his behavior in the hospital, the drugs affect his personality. He could never drink alcohol or use pain medication without you knowing about it because of his chemical makeup. He does not handle them well."

I had no idea of what we were in for. Nothing could have prepared us for the emotional roller-coaster ride our family would experience for the majority of Ted's life because of the greed and immoral practice of an unethical doctor.

For over a week, I could not leave him alone. Ted went through the horrors of paranoia, withdrawals, hallucinations, and nightmares. The most heartrending of all was the puzzled look on our little son's face when his daddy's mind was so confused he could not interact with him. I tried my best to console him by reassuring him that "Daddy was sick, but he will feel better soon."

After ten days, the nightmares ceased, withdrawal symptoms were less severe, and his paranoia was finally over. Ted had no memory of those days, but I shall never forget them. Even as I am recalling those very dark, heartrending days, tears are falling from my eyes.

My husband was an amazing man. For many years, he worked as an aircraft maintenance engineer and also had his own businesses. Ted was an excellent provider and extremely dependable. He was in his late thirties when he was declared disabled because of severe chronic arthritis after being injured on his job. However, that never stopped him from trying to support us. He continued to earn money by repairing cars. Ted suffered so much physically and emotionally, having gone through numerous surgeries. Despite his condition, he was positive and hopeful and had a good sense of humor. He loved his family. He was resourceful and smart with a photographic memory. He was a man of prayer and had a compassionate heart for people who were suffering. He had a lovely singing voice, played bass guitar, loved gospel music and jazz, and was an inventor and an excellent baker and cook—everyone loved his barbecue.

Despite the unpleasant seasons of life, the Lord blessed our marriage and family. We had a comfortable lifestyle, and we were blessed to raise three wonderful children. When the children became adults and left home, Satan began to work overtime to take my husband's mobility and mind. It was constant spiritual warfare to ensure he didn't succeed. Anyone who has dealt with dependent behavior knows it is a challenge to protect those who are afflicted with this disorder from self-destruction. Despite the challenges, the Lord always brought us through. He would get better and then would have another surgery, and the cycle of addiction would start all over again.

RESTORER

THERE WAS NEVER ANY QUESTION about our love for one another. Satan had used the circumstances beyond our control to emotionally and physically build a gap between us. A spirit of confusion had entered our home. We were not going in the same direction. He was weary with the demands of ministry, and I was weary with trying to justify his bizarre behavior to someone he had offended. There was a breakdown in communication, and neither of us was listening. We allowed Satan to separate us.

I knew who was using my husband, but I was tired. Ted said he had had enough and was leaving. When he left the house, I felt a sense of relief, but it wasn't long before I regretted letting things get out of control to the point he felt he had to leave. I was absolutely lost without him. I missed him and questioned how we had allowed things to get so out of hand. There is a misconception that pastors and ministers have a shield protecting them from the problems of life that many people go through. Nothing could be further from the truth. Ministers of the Lord Jesus Christ are faced with more satanic attacks, and they are more frequent and intense because they are God's representatives on the earth. Because ministers are under constant attack, intercessors are vital to the sustainability and success of any Christian ministry. These faithful spiritual warriors place a prayer covering over leaders and their families, pushing back the forces of darkness coming against the work of the Lord.

A couple of months after Ted left, I was led to move out of state so I took a sabbatical and left the church in the hands of one of the elders. The devil had me believing my marriage was over. I was brokenhearted. Next to God, the most important thing to me in this world was my family, and that was the one area in which Satan always used to try to drive me out of the will and presence of the

Lord. Hopelessness shadowed me. Every earthly thing that was important to me was suddenly gone: health, marriage, children, home, and ministry. After twenty-five years of feeling secure, with a family and ministry, I suddenly realized, that was only temporary security. My real security was my relationship with my heavenly Father. I felt bewildered by how my life had been so drastically changed in a matter of minutes. I clung to the only hope I had, Jesus. I became more aware of the Holy Spirit's presence and the angels that were with me. I was aware that my heavenly father was watching over me and protecting me. My faith in God and His Word sustained me through those very painful, lonely, mentally oppressive days. I prayed for the Lord to lead me to a spirit-filled church where I could heal and grow. I knew I needed spiritual fellowship, and one day, while driving down the street, I saw Victory Christian Center. I attended the Wednesday night service, and I knew God had answered my prayer. Soon, I was on the praise and worship team, in training to be a cell (Bible study) group leader, and enrolled in Bible school. The Holy Spirit convicted me of the spirit of unforgiveness shortly after I started attending the church. I contacted Ted to ask his forgiveness, and I told him I had forgiven him as well. That was the beginning of my restoration.

I continued my studies and worked faithfully in the church. In preparation for a mission trip to Tanzania, Africa, I went on a weekend retreat with thirty other missionary students. I had a burden for Africa and felt that God was calling me to that continent. I was alone and had resolved to spend the rest of my life in dedicated service to the Lord as an international missionary. But God was up to something completely different from what I had in mind.

During that weekend retreat, I had an encounter with God in the wee hours of the morning. After a long and exhausting day, I showered and went to bed.

Each night, I sensed the comforting presence of the Holy Spirit as I communed with the Lord. I drifted off to sleep, telling Him how much I loved Him and that I was willing to go wherever He needed me to go. Early in the morning before daybreak, I heard a gentle voice in my ear. My heavenly Father was saying, "Janice, if you love

Me, obey Me." I kept hearing the same words over and over until I was wide-awake. I lay there in the dark with my eyes open. Then He said, "You and your husband allowed the devil to take everything I gave you. I want you to call your husband and tell him what I said. You were married for twenty-five years, but you did not know how to be married. I want you both to go to biblical premarital counseling and to renew your vows."

I said, "Oh, Lord, please don't put me back into that bondage."

He said, "Have faith in Me, Janice."

I said, "But, Lord, too many things have been said. Too many people have been hurt."

God said, "I am working on his heart, just as I am working on yours."

I said, "Lord, I don't understand. I am willing to give You my life. I don't have a husband, children, or anyone but You. I am totally surrendered to Your will."

All of a sudden, I began to recall a conversation that took place in my apartment a couple of weeks prior to the retreat.

God sent a word of wisdom to me through another missionary student who was visiting me. We were discussing a different topic when she turned to me and said, "Janice, I know you are not going to like this, but God said you and your husband are going to get back together."

I responded by saying, "Girl, get out of here. That marriage is over."

While I thought about what I heard in my spirit, I tried to discern whether it was really the Lord or a deceiving spirit, trying to hinder me from going to Africa. However, I thought about the word of wisdom I received from the missionary student. I struggled with the idea of going back into a divided home. I had forgiven my husband, but only God could heal the marriage.

As soon as it was day, I put on some warm clothes, picked up my Bible, and walked around the campground, praying for God to change His mind. I had such mixed emotions. I wanted my marriage to be healed, but I wasn't convinced Ted was as dedicated as I was to laying his life down to follow Jesus. I said, "But, Lord, the marriage is dead."

Then the Holy Spirit instructed me to read Romans 4:17. I opened my Bible to the scripture, and it said, "As it is written, I have made thee a father of many nations before him whom he believed, even God, who quickeneth the dead, and calleth those things which be not as though they were."

That was God's response to my saying that the marriage was "dead." I was then certain God was going to restore everything. I knew it would certainly take a miracle to repair the damage we had done to our marriage, family, and ministry. I pondered my encounter with God for several days before I called Ted to tell him what God had said.

When I heard his voice, I knew he was still angry, and he said, "Jan, I am trying my best not to hate you."

I did not respond to what he said. All I could think about was being obedient to God. I said, "Ted, I called to tell you that God said we allowed the devil to steal everything He had given us." He was silent, so I said, "That's all I needed to tell you. Goodbye." I prayerfully waited and wondered what would happen next.

A couple of days later, I received a call from Ted, and he said, "Jan, I love you. I want to renew our vows. I want to come where you are."

I paused because at the time I still had a troubled heart.

He continued, "We need to be together. I want to come where you are."

The Lord had given me specific instructions about not being intimate with him until we renewed our vows. We needed God's blessings on our lives and on the lives of future generations.

Ten months after we lost everything, God restored us. Ted enrolled in Bible school. We spent the days together and ate together, but I slept at the home of a couple who attended school with us. It was a very difficult adjustment period for both of us because of the breach of trust. Only the Lord could heal our wounded hearts and renew our trust in each other. We had no doubt it was God's will to restore us, but it would take time. I was forced to walk by faith. My flesh did not want to line up with my faith because of the emotional wounds that were not completely healed. Ted and I attended biblical premarital counseling and renewed our vows to each other. Four months later, we felt led of the Holy Spirit to return to the West Coast to be closer to the family and to continue the ministry. The Lord miraculously healed our wounds and restored our souls, our love and devotion for one another, our family, and our ministry. He prospered us. Truly God proved to us He could breathe life into a dead marriage. "For with God nothing is impossible" (Luke1:37).

VICTOR'S CROWN

WHILE WE WERE OUT OF state, some of the ministers started pastoring, and others moved to other states but continued to serve under our ministry. Upon our return, we continued to minister in the same location. We refurbished the interior with new furniture and beautified the sanctuary. Three years later, I was led of the Lord to expand the Bible school. That would require a larger facility. The church was small and was located in a small town situated away from the main highway.

The Lord was calling me to train up men and women to spread the gospel. Ted and I prayed for the Lord to send a pastor to take over the church. It wasn't long before we met a couple who expressed an interest in continuing the church. We talked and prayed, and the Holy Spirit gave us peace about turning the ministry over to them. We prayed together, laying our hands on them, and gave them the key.

I moved on to fulfill the assignment God had given me. I rented a large office building in another city and established a school of ministry, Christ Living Word Bible Institute. I must admit it was very disappointing with only one student enrolled. I knew what God had said, so I stayed focused on what God called me to do and began training the student He sent. It wasn't long before the Lord began to add to the school. Students came from various Christian denominations and nondenominational churches throughout the Inland Empire. We had one very important rule that every student must abide by: "No discussion of denominations or church doctrines, only scriptures and Jesus Christ." It was amazing to witness the students' spiritual growth and passion for soul winning. A student from our school was working at a retail store when a customer had a heart attack. She was the first one to reach the customer, and she took authority over the spirit of death in the name of Jesus. God supernaturally delivered the woman from the clutches of death, and by the time the paramedics arrived, she was sitting up and talking. God used this willing vessel to stand between the woman and death. That is why God is having me write this book. Every believer is called to God's service. God is looking for someone He can work through to stand against the principalities, powers, and spiritual wickedness in this floundering world.

MISSION ACCOMPLISHED

THREE YEARS AFTER OPENING THE school of ministry, Ted said he wanted to move back to the South. I was not pleased with the idea of leaving because I was in the third year of building the school and there were only four months left before the students completed their studies. The Holy Spirit revealed to me a plan to conduct classes long distance. I really was not thrilled about leaving my students, but I felt God was doing something unusual. Ted said he wanted to fish and hunt. I knew I would be fishing for souls.

We sold our home in California and moved to the South. I had no idea why God had put this town in Ted's heart. But a couple of months later, the Lord revealed the purpose for sending us there. Ted enjoyed fishing and hunting and was very disappointed when he found out that, after sixty years, the fishing and hunting laws had changed. Ted was born in a small farming town approximately fifteen miles from where we bought a house. Several oldtimers remembered his family, so he was considered a hometown boy coming back home.

When the truck arrived with our furniture, people came from all directions, asking if they could help us unload the truck. I had never seen anything like that before. We didn't know it beforehand, but we had purchased a house in a neighborhood that was exclusively designated for whites. We paid cash for the house, so God opened the door for us to have that particular house.

Early one Sunday morning, we drove to the Methodist church Ted and his family had attended when he was growing up. Upon our arrival, we noticed the church was abandoned and vines completely covered it. We went to the Baptist church where he had attended church with his grandfather and grandmother. The church was 106 years old, and there was a handful of people still attending. We prayed and felt that God wanted us to worship with them. The pastor lived in another town and was hired to preach twice a month. He was a little wary of us at first when he heard I was an ordained minister and a pastor. However, God gave me favor with him. I was the first female to ever stand behind the pulpit and preach in the church. That was truly the favor of God. Baptist churches never allowed women in their pulpits, and this church was very traditional Baptist. When God's favor is upon your life, doors open that would otherwise be closed.

The pastor was a gracious man with a bellowing but beautiful singing voice. The people who attended the church had very little knowledge of scripture or how to locate scriptures in the Bible. The people never heard of the baptism of the Holy Spirit. A lady who attended the church had been blind all her life. Shortly before we arrived, she had eye surgery and was able to see for the first time in her life. She heard I was a teacher and asked if I would teach her to read the Bible. I began tutoring her and taught her about the baptism of the Holy Ghost, with the evidence of speaking in tongues according to Acts 19:1–6.

> And it came to pass, that while Apollos was at Corinth, Paul having passed through the upper coasts came to Ephesus: and finding certain disciples, He said unto them, Have ye received the Holy Ghost since ye believed? And they said unto him, We have not so much as heard whether there be any Holy Ghost. And he said unto them, Unto what then were ye baptized? And they said, unto John's baptism. Then said Paul, John verily baptized with the baptism of repentance, saying unto the people, that they should believe on him which should come after him, that is on Christ Jesus. When they heard this, they were baptized in the name of the Lord Jesus. And when Paul had laid his hands upon them, the Holy Ghost came on them; and they spake with tongues, and prophesied.

On a Monday morning, the sister arrived at my house for her reading lesson. I invited her into the den, and I stepped into another room. I heard a loud voice and someone speaking in tongues. The sister who came for her reading lesson was being filled with the Holy Ghost while she sat in the den alone. After she received the baptism of the Holy Ghost, she began to read the Bible fluently and able to quickly locate scriptures. I had never witnessed anything like it. It was an incredible manifestation of the real teacher, the Holy Spirit.

Ted and I loved serving the Lord. He taught the adult Sunday school class, and I was an associate minister. The pastor of the church was not too comfortable with Ted teaching about holiness and sanctification, so he would challenge him when we discussed these topics. It strained the relationship, and I knew the door to the church was closing. Because we were rural missionaries, we knew when our assignments were over. Now the Lord was calling us to establish a Truth Ministries Church in the town. Our garage was large, so we dedicated it to the Lord and starting having weekly Bible study. From the Bible study, we established the church.

BUILDING BRIDGES

I AM A VISIONARY WHO BELIEVES if God shows it to me, it can be done. The Holy Spirit was leading us to move the church. I rented a storefront and established a multipurpose facility. The population of the town was about 150 people, and there is no such thing as a secret in a town that small. Word had gotten around town that I was an ordained minister and I was opening up a building that had an unusual name. The name sounded more like a "juke joint." The word *juke* means disorderly in Gullah, meaning that these gathering spots were considered very rowdy for the era, frowned upon by many people during this time. People socialized with friends while eating, drinking, and gambling in these ramshackle buildings.[7]

I attended the town hall meeting to formally introduce myself and to share the plans I had to utilize the building. I informed them that I was opening a retail store to sell Christian books and music. From the proceeds of the sales, I would establish a youth work program, hire high school seniors, and train them to tutor other students. I would also train adult volunteers to tutor adults to help them learn to read or improve their literacy skills. To promote strong families, once a month, I would show inspirational family and Christian films. During holidays, when students were not in school, the facility would be used for youth activities, and beginner's piano classes would also be offered at the location. When I finished speaking, everyone was speechless and asked how they could help.

What I was proposing seemed impossible, but God had given the vision and blessed my husband and me to finance everything until sales picked up. We knew we were sent to minister the love of Jesus to the people in the town. We were honored that he had entrusted us with such an amazing assignment.

On the opening day of the business, the mayor and other city officials presented me with a gift and held a ribbon-cutting ceremony. Once again, God had given me favor.

Poverty is one demon spirit that plagues many families, particularly in the Southern states but more so among African American youth. What I was proposing would prepare them for employment after graduation, and I expected resistance about the youth work program. I was aware there was a county program that paid the wages of youth that were underprivileged. I submitted my application, but the woman who took my application said, "Yes, we have money for that program. But I will give it to anybody else but you."

Of course, that was not the response I expected. I said, "Why? I don't understand. I have presented you with the outline of the training, my business license, and copies of my credentials regarding my qualifications and experience as a human resources specialist and educator. What else do you need?" She said that she would needed to talk with her supervisor before she approved my application. I left the office knowing I wouldn't be approved for the program. But I knew God would make a way.

I printed flyers about a weekly morning prayer for women at the "J" Spot and posted them around town. I prayed and moved as directed by the Holy Spirit. The morning of the first prayer was divine. For the first time in the history of the town, white sharecroppers' wives and daughters and black sharecroppers' wives and daughters prayed together weekly at six in the morning. It was truly a miracle taking place. One of the women asked if we would pray for a particular young man who was very sick. I led them in prayer for him, and we believed the Lord would heal him. The Lord heard our prayers, and at the next prayer meeting, we were told that the young man was at home and doing fine.

When the mother of the young man found out that the prayer for her son had taken place at my business and I had led the women in prayer, she came to see me. This was the same woman who had refused my application for the funding for the youth work program. She thanked me for praying for her son and apologized for being rude and refusing my application. She said she felt such conviction for her behavior toward me that she resigned from that job and went to work for the bank. I didn't get approved for the program, but I won a friend and the Lord spared the life of a precious young man.

It was to be expected, the devil was not happy about anything that involved prayer or promoting the doctrines of the unity in Jesus Christ. A very prominent, highly influential person in the town heard we were praying for companies to move into the area to provide employment opportunities to residents, and I received a call to attend a meeting for business owners, where he expressed his opposition to any major industries doing business in the county, because it would affect the local retailers. I was instructed not to pray for companies to move into the county.

When you live in a small town, there's no need for advertising; just tell one person what you are going to do, and the whole town will know. Even the surrounding counties heard about the literacy program, and I received an invitation to attend a conference on literacy sponsored by the Arkansas State Literacy Council and the University of Fayetteville.

Not everyone was in favor of the literacy program or the youth work program providing jobs to high school seniors. People came out of the woodwork to try to usurp the work I was doing. Many of the black adults in the town never came into the building. They walked on the opposite side of the street. Most of the customers were white and from other small towns. They had heard there was a Christian book and music store in town. I had earned a reputation in the surrounding counties as a praying woman, and people came to the store for prayer. The Lord healed bodies and souls and restored marriages. The spirit of premature, mysterious deaths among young people in the town was broken.

The devil was so angry the people were seeking God and giving glory to the name of Jesus. He tried to frighten me. A demon spirit came into the store to try to bring a spirit of fear upon me. He came in the form of an old white man. I was alone, and when he entered the store, he looked around and said, "If you know what's good for you, you better get out of town."

I said, "God sent me here, and I am praying for God to heal your hearts and to deliver all of you from the spirit of hatred, that you repent and accept Jesus Christ, who is the only one who can give you peace of mind." While that poor man talked to me, I experienced intense grief and pity for him. The look in his eyes revealed a tormented, lost soul. He was a Klansman from another county who had tried to run me out of town.

I believe in creationism. According to the Bible, God made mankind in His image and in His likeness. Many professing Christians say they love God but despise Christians of different genders, denominations, skin pigmentations, economic statuses, languages, cultures, and beliefs. Jesus did not discriminate. He ministered to all whose hearts were open and receptive to the message of the kingdom of God.

Jesus revealed to John the Revelator what the true Body of Christ would look like: "After this I beheld, and lo, a great multitude, which no man could number, of all nations, and kindreds, and people, and tongues, stood before the throne, and before the Lamb, clothed with white robes, and palms in their hands" (Revelation 7:9).

All, nations, kindreds, tongues—it's pretty clear segregation and discrimination are not part of God's kingdom. Therefore, if these practices do not exist in God's kingdom, where did they originate? Obviously from the pit of hell.

Jesus prayed the will of His heavenly Father when He said, "Thy Kingdom come, Thy will be done in earth as it is in heaven" (Matthew 6:10).

Each of us has a responsibility to help usher in the answer to Jesus's prayer by rooting up, tearing down, and destroying false doctrines and ideologies that are devised to create division in the Body of Christ. I consider myself to be an end-time apostle, sent to promote unity in the Body of Christ.

LITERACY, GOD'S IDEA

I DISCOVERED THE MAJORITY OF THE children in the town had been diagnosed with some form of learning disability. Ninety-five percent of the children attending the local school were black. The Holy Spirit revealed to me it was not coincidental most of the children were on behavior modification medication and there was a demonic force at work. There was an ancient demonic stronghold set up to oppose quality educational opportunities for black children. The literacy work I was doing could significantly impact the town's revenue. Therefore, I thought it best that I relinquish my position as the president of the literacy program. I knew the powers that be were not going to fully endorse my program, so I chose a respected retired white schoolteacher to serve as president. Prior to my resignation, the literacy program had received $5,000 from the State Literacy Council. At a town hall meeting on literacy, the president of a local black university was the keynote speaker. He said, "I know it is God's will that everyone know how to read ..." (We all waited silently for his next statement.) "I know that because God wrote the Ten Commandments." I had never heard such a profound statement in defense of literacy. When people can read, it liberates them.

Jesus instructs us to "Search the scriptures; for in them ye think ye have eternal life. And they are they which testify of me" (John 5:39).

If you can't read, how can you search the scriptures? I suddenly realized why God put it on my husband's heart to move to this little town hidden behind a curtain of trees. Whenever God gives me an assignment, He also releases upon me a special anointing. It is the anointing that literally does the work. The anointing empowers you. Simply listen, and follow instructions. The late Dr. Paul Trulin wrote a book entitled *My Body, His life*. The message Dr. Trulin was conveying is when we present our bodies as a vessel for God's use, the Holy Spirit steps inside our physical bodies and does the work. That is how God works through us to accomplish His divine purpose in the earth. As we yield ourselves to His service, He takes up residence, and the work is energizing and almost effortless.

I was anointed and sent by God to the rural town as a "missionary." I was beginning to understand the real reason God had sent me to the town was to wake up those who slept and for the Holy Spirit to convict those who did not know the Jesus of the Bible. I was sent to publicly proclaim God's love for the people. The people lived in America, but they were tucked far away in the backwoods of rural America. God did not want the people to perish spiritually, socially, economically, or intellectually. He wanted the people to have the opportunity for an abundant life through Christ Jesus.

Our work was not in vain. God saved many souls, revealed hearts, mended race relations, and put a prayer covering over that little town. That was why Ted and I were sent!

GODLY MENTORING

THE MINISTRY GIFT OF THE apostle has been misunderstood or completely rejected by many mainstream denominations. Many believe there were only twelve men Christ anointed as apostles, "sent ones." They accept Paul and the names of other men who are recorded in the Bible as such but look suspiciously upon anyone, and particularly a female, whose works are evident of the calling as an apostle of Jesus Christ in the twenty-first century.

For those with the apostolic call, it means death to self and all worldly pleasures that feed the lust of the flesh, lust of the eyes, and the pride of life, exchanging all things, keeping their eyes fixed on Christ and Christ alone. It is to suffer sometimes to the despair of one's life. But despite all the suffering and self-denial, nothing satisfies or brings such unspeakable joy as knowing the Holy Spirit of God embodies you and you are in constant communion with the Lord, protected by angels as you carry out your assignment in the earth.

People ask, "How did you became an apostle?"

I tell them, "It was not my decision or even my desire. I was chosen and preordained by God before the foundation of the world to be an apostle. I had to make a conscious decision to step into my calling and to not be ashamed of the apostolic anointing upon my life. It takes real courage to do so, because you become a target for the forces of darkness, because you carry the light of the gospel inside of you."

The scriptures my apostolic calling is based upon are John 15:16–20 and Matthew 28:18–20.

> Ye have not chosen me, but I have chosen you, and ordained you, that ye should go and bring forth fruit,

> and that your fruit should remain: that whatsoever ye shall ask of the Father in my name, he may give it you. These things I command you, that ye love one another. If the world hate you, ye know that it hated me before it hated you. If ye were of the world, the world would love his own: but because ye are not of the world, but I have chosen you out of the world, therefore the world hateth you. Remember the word that I said unto you, The servant is not greater than his lord. If they have persecuted me, they will also persecute you; if they have kept my saying, they will keep yours also.
>
> And Jesus came and spake unto them saying, All power is given unto me in heaven and in earth. Go ye therefore, and teach all nations, baptizing them in the name of the Father, and of the Son, and of the Holy Ghost: Teaching them to observe all things whatsoever I have commanded you: and lo, I am with you always, even unto the end of the world Amen.

The call was undeniable. I had a mandate on my life, and the only reason I live is to fulfill it. I expected there would be a great deal of persecution from my brothers and sisters in Christ. I had to resist the spirit of fear that was trying to deceive me into disobedience by denying the apostolic call. I am thankful for a godly woman who recognized the call to ministry on my life when I was a young woman. Her name was the late Mother Janie Blake. She was my mentor. I was a young woman when she appointed me to be the president of the District Young Women Christian Council. Most of the women were older than I, and they gave me a very difficult time. I called her to complain about the trouble they were giving me, and I told her I wanted to resign from the position. She said, "No, baby, God told me to put you there." She would not let me quit. She was an amazing, anointed, wise woman. Mother Blake and the late Elder C. J. Blake were apostles of the Lord Jesus Christ.

They held prayer meetings in their home. Mother Blake established the first Pentecostal church in Riverside, California, in the early 1930s. She spent hours with me, sharing about the work of the ministry and how she received the baptism of the Holy Ghost. Whenever I traveled on a ministry assignment, I'd call her and share what I was doing. Upon returning home from an out-of-state assignment, I would visit her in her home and share with her the wonderful adventurous assignment. We would talk for hours about the work of the ministry. I was like a sponge soaking up her spiritual wisdom and experience. One day, we were sitting in her home, talking about the Lord, when suddenly, the presence of God fell upon her, and she began to quiver and shake. She held her hands out to me and said, "Here take it!" God's presence fell upon me, and her anointing was transferred to me. She was a "jewel," one of God's special daughters. At ninety-six, the Lord took her from this world into His glorious presence that she might rest from her labor. I consider myself extremely blessed to have had this great woman apostle as my spiritual mentor and precious friend.

Growing up in the church, I never heard of anyone other than the apostle Paul and the twelves disciples of Christ being called "apostles." Pastors were the primary preachers in the churches I attended. Of course, there were evangelists, but I don't recall ever hearing anyone addressed as an apostle of Jesus Christ.

I realized very early in ministry the importance of prevailing prayer and earnestly studying the Bible. The spirit of evangelism rested upon me. I had a burning passion for soul winning and to reach people with the Good News of salvation through Christ. I was called to reach the people who did not go to church and those who had not heard the gospel of Jesus Christ, so I proclaimed the gospel in vacant lots under trees in front of grocery stores. I ordered Bibles and went house to house to offer the people in the community free Bibles and to pray for their needs. I made sandwiches and went to the parks to feed, teach, and pray for the homeless. I witnessed incredible miracles in response to the prayer of faith and the laying on of hands in the name of Jesus Christ.

I had my victories, but also many heartaches, mental battles, and physical assaults. Because of my conviction to defend the scriptures and preach the gospel of Jesus Christ of the Bible at any cost, I've been hated, so was Jesus; assaulted, so was Jesus; cast out of churches, so was Jesus; threatened, so was Jesus; scorned, so was Jesus; lied on, so was Jesus; used, so was Jesus; betrayed, so was Jesus; abandoned, so was Jesus; and laughed at, so was Jesus. But He was guiltless and sinless. I was born in sin and shaped in iniquity, wretched and without hope until Jesus lifted me out of the miry clay. Therefore, I am willing to uphold the torch of this glorious gospel of redemption and everlasting life through Jesus Christ, until I finish my course or my Lord returns.

When I think about what Christ suffered, I've suffered nothing, compared to Him. When I think about the humiliation and the harsh treatment I received, it is nothing compared to what Jesus went through. Jesus said, "Verily, verily, I say unto you the servant is not greater than his lord; neither he that is sent greater than he that sent him" (John 13:16).

In Matthew 5:10–12, Jesus said,

> Blessed, are they which are persecuted for righteousness' sake: for theirs is the kingdom of heaven. Blessed are ye when men shall revile you, and persecute you, and shall say all manner of evil against you falsely, for my sake. Rejoice, and be exceeding glad: for great is your reward in heaven: for so persecuted they the prophets which were before you.

I knew from the beginning of my ministry that I was called to raise up, equip, and train men and women for Christian ministry. I knew when they completed their training, they would move on, and the Lord would bring others. I learned very early in ministry that I was never to get too attached to those I had been sent to minister to or to take things personally. Over the years, I have been conditioned to bear the betrayal, accusations, and abuse that go along with an "apostolic calling" because I am female. The precious Holy Spirit always comforts, strengthens, and sustains me.

Jesus addressed this issue of being hated and disliked because of the message we carry. He said, "He that is of God heareth God's words, ye therefore hear them not, because, ye are not of God" (John 8:47).

The Holy Ghost endows spirit-filled believers with spiritual gifts. The "gift of discerning of spirits" is a revelation gift that provides spiritual insight and eyesight. Discerning of spirits is the supernatural ability given by the Holy Ghost in order that the believer may perceive the source of a spiritual manifestation and determine whether it is of God (Acts 10:30–35), the devil (Acts 16:16–18), man (Acts 8:18–23), or the world (1 Corinthians 3:1–3).

The Spirit of God brings the anointing, authority, miracles, wonders, love, prophecy, salvation, and deliverance. The Spirit of the world is manifested by the love of recognition, pride of accomplishment, strife, wrath, offense, manipulation, and greed. The spirit of the devil brings strife, division, debates, hypocrisy, immorality, and disobedience. The Body of Christ has been given every spiritual gift needed to complete the work of evangelizing the whole world. Our job as the Body of Christ is to conquer territory occupied by the devil. The devil has hindered the propagation of the Gospel of Jesus Christ by blinding the eyes of the church to Christ's inclusion of women in His army in whatever position He desires. Believers must be careful of spiritual deception.

Scripture warns the church in Colossians 2:8, "Beware lest any man spoil you through philosophy and vain deceit, after the tradition of men, after the rudiments of the world, and not after Christ."

ONE SET OF FOOTPRINTS

IN 2013, MY HUSBAND, PASTOR Ted Turner, left behind the cares of this old world to rest from his labor in the presence of the Lord. I continue to carry on the work, endeavoring to finish my course strong. I was absolutely lost without my precious husband, best friend, confidant, and colaborer and the father of my children. After many years of running from the call of a preacher, he accepted his call as a pastor in 2010. Three months prior to his surrender to God's will on his life, he woke up one morning and could not move. He had a compressed spinal cord. The prognosis was very poor. The doctor said he may never walk again or turn his head from side to side, and he would be in pain for the rest of his life. Numerous times, Ted had been healed. We knew the Lord Jesus was a miracle worker. Once again, we were believing and trusting in Him to perform another miracle healing in Ted's body. We read, believed, meditated, and stood on Mark 11:22–24:

> And Jesus answering saith unto them, Have faith in God. Verily I say unto you that whosoever shall say unto this mountain, Be thou removed, and be thou cast into the sea; and shall not doubt in his heart, but shall believe that those things which he saith will come to pass; he shall have whatsoever he saith. Therefore I say unto you, What things soever ye desire when ye pray, believe that ye receive them, and ye shall have them.

We agreed in Jesus's name, not only would Ted walk after the surgery, but he would turn his head from side to side, and there would be no more pain. After the surgery, the doctor came out to speak with me. He said, "Your husband is doing well. I tried to put eight screws in his neck, but I was only able to get seven to go in."

When I heard the number seven, I had no doubt God had performed another miracle. Seven is God's divine number for completeness. My husband's recovery was miraculous. He had little pain following the surgery. He could move his head from side to side. Not only did he walk, but he started driving again. He was completely free from pain and pain-pill dependency. God gave us three glorious years of divine health, joy, productivity, and supernatural blessings. During those three years, people received Christ and were healed, and the Lord added to the church. God used Ted's supernatural healing to increase the faith of the people in the congregation and others who heard about his healing.

In 2012, Ted had a compelling desire to spend Thanksgiving with our oldest son in Louisiana. I was unable to go because I was caring for an elderly member of our congregation and had no one to care for her. Ted flew to Louisiana, and on Thanksgiving Day, Hurricane Isaac pummeled the state with such a force it caused massive destruction. Ted's immune system was suppressed by medications he had taken for arthritis. When he finally arrived home, I noticed he didn't look well. He came down with a bacterial infection and passed away a few months later. After my husband went to be with the Lord, I was extremely lonely. I had known him for over fifty years. He was my best friend, and we were married for forty-five years. He was the father of my children and colaborer in Christ.

Several months after Ted went to be with the Lord, I had to make a very difficult decision regarding the church. It was during that time I became so much more aware of how intertwined Ted and I were spiritually. We often talked about how God put us together for ministry and how effective we were as a team. I missed talking and praying with him. Half of my life was stripped from me when Ted was no longer by my side. But I knew I had work to do and was determined with God's strength and the counsel of the Holy Spirit, I would continue on and finish my course. It took four years before I was emotionally and spiritually ready to continue my journey without Ted. Because there is an unseen battle between the kingdom of heaven and the kingdom of hell, there will always be spiritual warfare in ministry, but there is more intense spiritual warfare when worshipping in a facility that is not exclusively dedicated and consecrated for the work of the ministry. I learned from personal experience that spiritual fasting is a powerful Christian weapon, and every Sunday, we fasted until after the worship service. Fasting crucifies the flesh and strengthens the spirit man. We sanctified the atmosphere before the worship service by praying in the spirit, taking authority, binding and casting out demonic spirits from the place, and welcoming the Holy Spirit.

One Sunday morning, I arrived to discover a new lock on the gate, and I had not been notified or given a key. I knew it was an attack of the devil to frustrate me, but I was there early enough to be able to reach someone before time for service, I hoped. After several unsuccessful attempts, I finally reached one of the employees. I said, "This is Rev. Turner. The lock has been changed on the gate, and I was not notified or given a key. I need to set up for service at nine o'clock."

She said, "Oh, I am so sorry, Rev. Turner. The lock was changed Friday because we were having problems with people from the alcohol program entering the facility without permission. I had planned to meet you early this morning to give you a key, but I am sick and overslept."

I said, "I understand, but people will be arriving for service shortly, and we need to get in so we can set up."

Fortunately, she did not live far from the facility, and we were able to get in and set up before anyone arrived. I had to preach, so I did not allow my mind to dwell upon the matter. I had a job to do. In the past, we had pressed through many difficulties, knowing God had led us to the location, but October and December were especially difficult for us, because they would heavily decorate the area where we held our services with secular decorations, and we had to work especially hard to prepare for the service. We had to remove everything and replace it after service. During Easter and the Christmas season, we prepared a free hot meal for the residents of the community and ministered to them about the significance of the birth, death, and resurrection of Jesus Christ. In response to the messages, many received Jesus.

Our membership was rather small, and the majority were older. The younger members were sometimes not able to attend church because they worked on Sunday. This presented a real challenge for me because I could not do all the work by myself. After much prayer, it became clear that God was leading me to close the church down at this location. The rent was very reasonable where we were, and we did not have the financial means to pay rent on another place. I met with the members and shared what the Lord was leading me to do. I told them, "I believe our time here is up. We don't have the help to set up and tear down for services each Sunday, and the inconsideration of the staff to inform me of a lock change and the failure to provide me with a key to the gate serve as an indicator that they want us to move."

My heart was extremely heavy as I looked into the faces of the precious people I pastored. Some cried, and I could see the disappointment on their faces. I knew without God's Spirit, the work would be in vain. Only He could provide the help we needed. We prayed together, and I gave them a list of churches in the area to visit. I prayerfully listed pastors who were spirit-filled, sound teachers of the Word and demonstrated godly character. It was such a difficult task, but I realized Ted and I were undershepherds; Jesus is the chief shepherd. By faith, I had to trust He would guide them to the right place to worship.

The following Sunday, I visited two of the churches I served as the overseer and started visiting other churches in the community. When it comes to the work of the ministry, especially church ministry, prayer is the fundamental foundation. Whenever I visited a morning worship service, I would inquire about the time of the prayer service for the purpose of attending. I discovered churches with over ten thousand in attendance have a small remnant of people praying for that ministry. This is a sad fact in most churches in America. No wonder pastors, their families, and their ministries are being ruthlessly attacked by the devil. There is a great falling away. Deadly diseases are attacking the bodies of God's people, all because people are not praying. There is little or no corporate prayer in the churches. But there is hope. God will respond when people pray.

In 2 Chronicles 7:14–15, God said, "If my people which are called by my name, shall humble themselves, and pray, and seek my face, and turn away from their wicked ways; then will I hear from heaven, and will forgive their sin, and will heal their land. Now mine eyes shall be open, and mine ears attent unto the prayer that is made in this place."

God is calling the church back to the altar. He is waiting for us to prostrate ourselves before Him, crying out for salvation, mercy, and grace.

I am thankful God called me into the apostolic ministry. The things I suffered served to equip me with the tenacity to endure hardness as a good soldier and established my total dependency upon God. Unlike others who have kept a numerical record of decisions for Christ, healings, and deliverances, I have not done so. My main focus is that those whose lives I have touched have their names written in the Lamb's Book of Life. Many times, the people I ministered to did not know my name, but after meeting me, they knew the name of Jesus. I emphasized to those I taught in the schools of ministry the utmost importance of teaching and preaching about the God of Abraham, Isaac, and Jacob; His Son, Jesus Christ, of the Holy Scriptures; and the kingdom of God.

Apostle Paul cautioned the church against preaching another gospel. He said,

> I marvel that ye are so soon removed from him that called you into the grace of Christ unto another gospel. Which is not another; but there be some that trouble you and would pervert the gospel of Christ. But though we, or an angel from heaven, preach any other gospel unto you than that which we have preached unto you, let him be accursed. And we said before, so say I now again, If any man preach any other gospel unto you than that ye have

> received, let him be accursed. For do I now persuade men, or God? Or do I seek to please men? For if I yet pleased men, I should not be the servant of Christ. But I certify you, brethren that the gospel which was preached of me is not after man. For I neither received it of man, neither was I taught it but by the revelation of Jesus Christ. (Galatians 1:6–12)

Because we are our heavenly Father's children, He delights in our reverence of Him as holy, almighty, and wise. When we search the scriptures seeking His instructions for even the smallest matter, it pleases God because it reveals to Him our complete trust and dependency upon Him. Our world is in a critical state. There's no hope without God's intervention. The root cause of everything going on in the world is one thing, sin, the sickness of human souls. Souls need healing. Nothing but the blood of Jesus has the power to cleanse a sin-sick soul.

In the Great Commission, Jesus gave the church an assignment to complete before He returns. Our primary focus as followers of Christ is to fulfill it.

> And Jesus came and spake unto them, saying, All power is given unto me in heaven and in earth. Go ye therefore, and teach all nations, baptizing them in the name of the Father and of the Son, and of the Holy Ghost: Teaching them to observe all things whatsoever I have commended you: and, lo, I am with you always, even unto the end of the world. A'men. (Matthew 28:16–20)

Debates over gender roles are not part of the assignment. The Body of Christ has been deceived by the devil. God's will for humankind is for them to survive the evil of this world and to spend eternity with Him in His heavenly kingdom.

God spoke through the prophet Joel to call His people to battle!

> Proclaim ye this among the Gentiles; Prepare war, wake up the mighty men, let all the men of war draw near; let them come up: Beat your plowshares into swords, and your pruning hooks into spears: let the weak say, I am strong.

> Assemble yourselves together round about thither cause thy mighty ones to come down, O Lord. Let the heathen be wakened and come up to the valley of Jehoshaphat for there will I sit to judge all the heathen around about. Put ye in the sickle, for the harvest is ripe: come, get you down; for the press is full the fats overflow; for their wickedness is great. Multitudes, multitudes in the valley of decision: for the day of the Lord is near in the valley of decision. The sun and the moon shall be darkened, and the stars shall withdraw their shining. The Lord also shall roar out of Zion, and utter his voice from Jerusalem; and the heavens and earth shall shake; but the Lord will be the hope of his people, and the strength of the children of Israel. (Joel 3:9–4)

The Lord is calling His church back to its original purpose, leading people to Calvary's cross to seek Jesus, where they will be free from all guilt and shame, lifting their eyes to the Lamb of God, who restores them back to their heavenly Father.

Perhaps you are a wounded warrior who has questioned your identity in Christ and what God is calling you to do. My prayer is that this book has been a source of insight, healing, hope, and inspiration. Perhaps you were afraid to step into your apostolic calling, but now you are no longer afraid. Now you are certain that your God is going before you and will strengthen you. You know the Lord has assigned warring angels to surround you and protect you, and they will go before you to fight back the forces of darkness that will try to stop you. God will defeat all your enemies!

Jesus prayed to the Father to give His followers another comforter.

> And I will pray the Father, and he shall give you another Comforter, that he may abide with you for ever; Even the Spirit of truth; whom the world cannot receive, because it seeth him not, neither knoweth him, but ye know him, for he dwelleth with you, and shall be in you. (John 14:16, 17)

God assures the people who put their absolute trust in Him of His great faithfulness to them through Isaiah His faithful prophet.

> Hast thou not known? Hast thou not heard, that the everlasting God, the Lord, the Creator of the ends of the earth, fainteth not, neither is weary? There is no searching of his understanding. He giveth power to the faint; and to them that have no might he increaseth strength. Even the youths shall fall; But they that wait upon the Lord shall renew their strength; they shall mount up with wings as eagles; they shall run, and not be weary; and they shall walk, and not faint. (Isaiah 40:28–31)

The same spirit of Almighty God that quickened Jesus's lifeless body in the grave will quicken your mortal body. He is breathing even now new life into you, raising you up to soar high above the clouds of adversity, to a level of unshakable confidence in the finished work of Jesus Christ that was accomplished on the cross at Calvary.

King David reigned forty years over Israel. His enemies constantly threatened, taunted, and fought against him, but David knew the battles were God's, not his. I encourage you to remember this and adopt David's confession of faith as your own by saying, "The Lord is on my side: I will not fear: what can man do unto me?" (Psalm 118:6).

MY PRAYER FOR YOU

OUR FATHER WHICH ART IN heaven,

I ask that You fill, empower, and release a fresh new anointing upon every person reading this book in the name of Jesus. Fan the fire of evangelism that it may burn so bright within them that souls will be drawn to them. Make their tongues a ready pen, drawing the path that sinners may follow to find Jesus. Spirit of the living God, guide Your people, teach them, and comfort them. Lead them not into temptation. Keep them from the evil in the world. Release a spirit of unending joy and excitement upon them, knowing that their names are written in the Lamb's Book of Life. Empower them with keen discernment, prevailing faith, and relentless confidence, in the power and authority of the name of Jesus Christ, our Lord and soon coming King. Amen.

APPENDIX

MIRACLE-WORKING POWER OF GOD

THE GOD WE SERVE IS continuing to perform supernatural miracles and provide divine protection for those who put their trust in Him. Jesus Christ is the same today, yesterday, and forever (Hebrews 13:8). With God, all things are possible" (Matthew 19:26).

An unbelieving generation must see unquestionable miracles to believe God is alive, He is the Creator, He loves them, and His thoughts are always good toward them. These are just a few testimonies of creative miracles, divine interventions, and supernatural deliverances I've witnessed personally. To God be the glory!

Spina Bifida Healed
A man and his wife heard a testimony of someone whom God healed in our ministry. By faith, they brought their newborn baby girl, believing God to heal her of spina bifida. I set my faith with their faith in the healing power of Jesus, anointed the baby with oil, laid hands on the baby, and prayed the prayer of faith. Two years later, a couple with a small girl came to see me. It was the parents and the little girl God sent for prayer two years earlier. Jesus had healed the child of spina bifida, and she was walking and was perfectly healthy. Praise Jesus!

Toddler Miraculously Healed
One of the ministers of the church brought her two-year-old nephew to a weekend prayer and fasting shut-in. He was frail and weak. He had failure-to-thrive syndrome, an ear infection, and a

severe cold; was severely dehydrated; had a temperature ranging from 102 to 103 Fahrenheit, and hadn't eaten in three days. He could not sit up, walk, or talk. She laid the baby on a blanket in front of the altar as we all knelt and prayed. Early in the morning, before daybreak, we sensed the presence of the Lord among us. The power of God touched the baby's body, and the fever broke. A couple of hours after I returned home, I received a call from Minister Ann, telling me her nephew walked into her room and asked for food. Jesus supernaturally healed the child. Glory hallelujah!

Divine Protection / Supernatural Intervention

Minister Linda and I were working in the church, attempting to remove a steel pipe that stretched from one side of the sanctuary to the other near the ceiling. I didn't know it at the time, but it was an electrical conduit with a live wire running through it. I climbed up a six-foot metal ladder and removed the screws from one end of the pipe while she stood on the concrete floor holding the ladder and the other end of the pipe. I saw a wire coming out of the pipe, cut the wire, and miraculously the wire cutters flew out of my hand, sparks started flying, and the room filled with smoke. We had no idea of the miracle God had performed until my husband returned and told us it was a miracle we were still alive. I had cut a 220-volt live electric wire while standing on a metal ladder. God protected us from unseen danger, sparing our lives (Psalm 91).

Child Delivered from Behavior Modification Drugs

A lady told me her son had been on behavior modification drugs for two years, but she did not want him on them anymore. She was believing God to deliver her son. We met with the principal, school nurse, and director of food services to discuss alternatives to implement in place of medication. After much discussion, they agreed to give me a month to see if what I proposed would work; otherwise, the child would not be allowed to return to school unless he took the medicine. We prayed, and the Holy Spirit directed us to make changes in his diet and sleep habits. His mother and I discussed eliminating sugary foods and beverages. She would prepare healthy lunches and make sure he had plenty of sleep. We believed God to intervene on behalf of the family. We prayed with the child, and after a month, his behavior had improved so much that his grades went up. They placed him in a regular fifth-grade classroom. What a mighty God we serve!

Chains of Death Broken

I received a call from a pastor's wife, informing me that her husband had suffered a stroke and he was in a rehabilitation center and not doing too well. The Lord led me to go visit him. When I arrived at the facility, his wife met me and directed me to his room. When I entered the room, his eyes had set and he was not breathing. I went to the side of his bed, called his name, and told him to come back. His eyes came down, and he began to breathe. His wife walked into the room just before he started breathing and began to call for help. God raised the pastor up and put him back into his pulpit. Holy, holy is the Lord!

Witchcraft Broken

A mother brought her teenage daughter for me to pray for her because the girl was unable to eat. I read salvation scriptures to her. She repented of her sin and gave her life to Jesus. I gave her a Bible and scriptures to read. She started coming to church, but she still was not eating. Months went by, and she was nothing but skin and bones. She became extremely weak, and she was hospitalized for them to insert a feeding tube to nourish her. When she returned home, she wasn't any better. While I was praying for her one day, the Holy Spirit revealed to me that her condition was not a physical illness; it was spiritual. He told me it was witchcraft. I went to her home to see her. She was so weak she was bedridden. I asked her a few questions about whether she had been in any conflicts with anyone. She shared that she had and described the incidents that had taken place. I then shared what the Holy Spirit had revealed to me about the spirit of witchcraft that was trying to destroy her. I told the girl and her mother that God was going to deliver her. I prayed in the spirit, and the Holy Ghost revealed what spirits were operating. In the name of Jesus Christ and in His authority, I commanded the spirits to loose her and commanded them to leave in Jesus's name. She was immediately set free. She began to eat. God instantly delivered her. Luke 4:18 tells us Jesus said, "He has sent me to set at liberty the captive." Hallelujah!

Amazing Grace

A young girl who sometimes attended our church called me late one night to tell me she had run away from home because her mother had beaten her. I drove to where she was and took her to my house. I called the local police department to inform them of the incident and to report the child was at my home. The next day, the mother of the child arrived at the church looking for her daughter. She was furious. I kept trying to convince her not to hurt the child or harm me. But she was beyond reasoning with. When the child saw her, she started holding on to the back of my blouse, begging me to protect her from her mother. This woman was heavyset, and she used her huge body to push me from one side of the sanctuary wall to the other. The child was screaming and crying as I shielded her from her mother. The woman angrily threatened and cursed at me as she swung her huge fists and arms at me. A member of the church heard the commotion and called the police. The mother was restrained, and the officers took the mother and the child to the police station. I later learned the mother moved with all eight of her children after the incident.

Several months later, I received a call from one of the ministers informing me that the woman who had assaulted me suffered a stroke a few months after the incident. Three years later, while I was visiting the first church we planted, to my surprise, the woman who assaulted me was there. By the grace and mercy of God, the woman's speech and mobility had been restored. She had given her life to the Lord. She was indeed a different woman from the one I'd encountered three years earlier. She was humble, and you could see the peace of God upon her countenance. She wept and apologized for assaulting me. God wanted this woman and her children not to perish but to experience His love and grace. Glory to God!

Life Giver

I was sitting in my home and was prompted by the Holy Spirit to call Minister Lupe. When she answered the phone, she was at the hospital, sitting at the bedside of her daughter, who was twenty-five weeks into her pregnancy and hemorrhaging. Both the mother's and baby's lives were in danger. The doctor finally made a decision to take the baby. He told the mother that if the baby survived the delivery, he would be placed on her chest and would most likely die because he was not fully developed. He also warned her that if he did survive, he would have many challenges. We prayed and sought our heavenly Father on behalf of the mother and the child.

God heard our prayers. The baby weighed one pound ten ounces when he was born. Today, he is a healthy seven-year-old boy who is excelling in school, with none of the complications doctors projected. To God be the glory!

Divine Guidance

A doctor discovered a large tumor in my daughter's chin. They informed us that the only way to treat the tumor was to remove it.

The doctor said, "Because of the location of the tumor, I will have to remove all your lower teeth, remove your chin, and graft in bone from your hip."

We looked at each other and said, "No way."

We thanked him, and I told her we were going to believe God for her healing. We sought the Lord for guidance and asked Him to heal her. She went to visit her dentist, and he referred her to a specialist in another city. When he looked at the x-ray and examined her, he said, "Oh, this is easy. We will just go in and suck that tumor out. I've done many of these."

She had the surgery, healed rapidly without leaving a scar. Jeremiah 33:3 says, "Call on me I will answer ..." Hallelujah!

ENDNOTES

1 Eddie Hyatt, 2014, www.charismamag.com/spirit/church-ministry/20285-can-women-be-apostles.

2 World Population Clock, www.worldmeters.info/world-population.

3 pewforum.org/2016/12/19 global-christianity-exec.

4 Av1611.com/kjbp/kjv-dictionary/ooil.html.

5 Av1611.com/kjbp/kjv-dictionary/perpetual.html.

6 av611.com/kjbp/kjv-dictionary/rest.html.

7 www.sweetgeorgiasjukejoint.com/history.html.

My Father Clifford Artry

My Mother Hattie Artry

Our Family

(L-R) Clifford, Terrance,
Ted, Angela, Janice

Uncle James & Aunt Solena Wall

Uncle Premon & Aunt Levada Hankins

Ruby, Charles & Janice

Spiritual Mentors

District Missionary Mother Janie Blake

Janice, Dr. Morris and Mrs. Theresa Cerullo
World Evangelism

Siblings

Rozina & Jean

Elaine, Ernestine, Catherine

Luther (Sonny)

Grand Children

Jasmine & Amber

Terrance II, Erynn-Dnae

Clifford Jr.(CJ), Tiffany, Ashley

Ancestors

My grandmother (Hattie's Mother), Margaret Thomas Chandler Henderson; Mississippi, Riverside, CA (Lineage Esan Nigerian)

Ancestors Great Grandmother Bettie Stephens & Grandparents Richard & Lucresia Artry (Red River County, Shawnee Town, Indian Territory)

CPSIA information can be obtained
at www.ICGtesting.com
Printed in the USA
LVHW030329150221
679323LV00004B/243